MATHEMATICS
ILLUSTRATED DICTIONARY

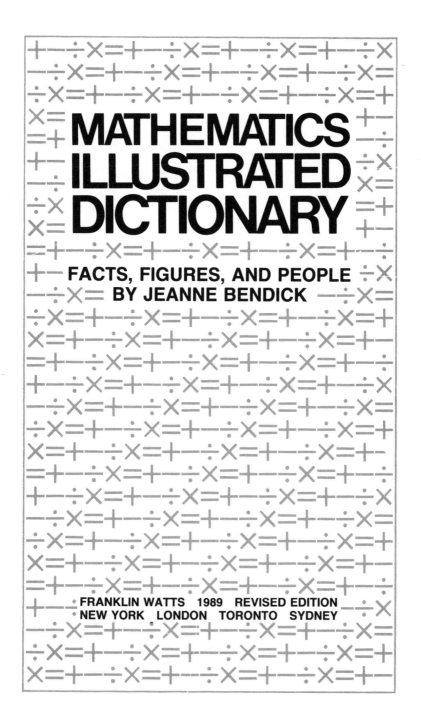

MATHEMATICS ILLUSTRATED DICTIONARY

FACTS, FIGURES, AND PEOPLE
BY JEANNE BENDICK

FRANKLIN WATTS 1989 REVISED EDITION
NEW YORK LONDON TORONTO SYDNEY

Photographs courtesy of:
The Bettmann Archive: pp. 25, 34 (right), 41, 66, 78, 87,
93, 98, 106, 120, 134, 145, 153, 173, 174, 181 (left), 217;
IBM: pp. 34 (left), 168;
Yerkes Observatory: pp. 42, 89, 130; National Museum of Naples: p. 75;
New York Public Library Picture Collection: pp. 136, 181 (right), 196;
Burndy Library: p. 155; Los Alamos National
Laboratory: p. 231.

Library of Congress Cataloging-in-Publication Data
Bendick, Jeanne.
Mathematics illustrated dictionary : facts, figures, and people /
by Jeanne Bendick. — Rev. ed.
p.   cm.
Summary: A dictionary of mathematical terms from abacus to zone.
Includes a section of tables, symbols, abbreviations, and formulas.
ISBN 0-531-10664-0
1. Mathematics—Dictionaries, Juvenile. [1. Mathematics—
Dictionaries.] I. Title.
QA5.B4 1989   89-8977   CIP   AC
510'.3—dc20

To math teachers
everywhere

My thanks to Pierre Fabinski
for all his help and his suggestions,
and to Marcia O. Levin
who did the original edition with me.

CONTENTS

MATHEMATICS
ILLUSTRATED DICTIONARY

HOW TO USE
THIS BOOK

Most terms appear in alphabetical order rather than under a general heading. For example, acute angle, obtuse angle, and right angle appear under A, O, and R, though they are mentioned and cross-referenced under the general description of angle.

Cross-references that are important to an understanding of any term are usually given in *italics*. If you are unfamiliar with modern mathematics terms, it might be helpful to begin by looking up some of these words below, which appear over and over again, though not always as cross-references.

arithmetic laws	line segment
axis	notation system
number line	numeral
base of a numeration	operation
system	perpendicular
binary system	plane
coordinates	point
diameter	polygon
endpoint	sentence, mathematical
inequality	set
integer	space figure
intersection	

If you cannot find a word, it may be listed in a slightly different form. For example, you might be looking for "approximate" and find your description under "approximation."

Some terms are commonly shortened. "Positive" may refer to positive integers; "primes" refer to prime numbers; "solids" mean solid or space figures.

Tables, symbols, abbreviations, and formulas are at the back of the book, but they are also cross-referenced with the text. For example, the description of a circle will also give you the page numbers where you will find formulas related to circles; the description of the metric system will refer you to the pages where you will find metric system tables.

A

A. The capital letter A is used to name a *point;*

an *angle;*

the *vertex* of a *polygon;*

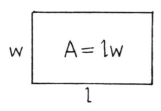

a *set* of *elements:* A = (1, 2, 3);

in formulas: A = lw;

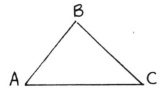

in the abbreviation for acre, area, altitude, or other things.

a. The lowercase a is used as a *variable* in a *formula;*

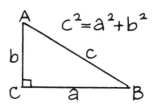

to represent the measure of the side of a *polygon;* to name a *line;*

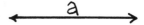

in *equations,* as a *variable:* 2a = 18; to express general *properties.* For example, since the order of adding two numbers does not change the sum, the property may be stated: a + b = b + a.

abacus (AB-a-cus). An ancient calculating machine still

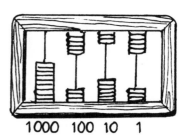

1000 100 10 1

used in some parts of the world to aid in arithmetic computation. It is made of beads strung on wires fastened into a frame. In elementary school it is used for teaching *place value*. Each wire has a place value, and each bead has a *number value*.

Abel, (AY-bel) **Niels,** 1802–1829. A Norwegian mathematician who helped develop group theory. He showed that the *roots* of a fifth-degree *equation* cannot be expressed by means of *radicals* in terms of the *coefficient* of the equation. He also did work with the binomial expansion and convergence, all before he died at age twenty-seven.

Abelian group. See *commutative group*.

abscissa (ab-SISS-a). The first number of an *ordered pair* of

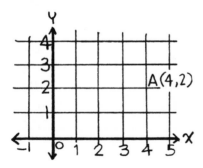

numbers called the *coordinates*, which are used to locate a *point* on a *plane*. In the picture, 4 is the abscissa of point A in the plane. It is also the distance from the *y-axis*. Point A's position, or its address, is (4, 2). See *ordinate*.

absolute constant. See *constant*.

absolute difference. The difference between two numbers when the smaller number is subtracted from the larger. The absolute difference between 8 and 5 is 3.

absolute error. In measuring, the difference between *true length* and *measured length*. Also called the *error of measurement*.

absolute unit. A unit that has an unchanging value at all times and in all situations. The *centimeter* has been set as the absolute unit of length, the *gram* as the absolute unit of mass, and the *second* as the absolute unit of time. Other units are based on this *cgs system* which is the metric system. The cgs (centimeter, gram, and second) system is used for "small" measures.

Larger measures use the mks (meter, kilogram, and second) system.

absolute value. The absolute value of a number, whether it is positive or negative, is always positive. For example, the absolute value of zero is zero. Absolute value can be shown on the *number line* as the distance from the *point* associated with the number to the zero point. The symbol

ABSOLUTE VALUE OF 2

for the absolute value of a number is vertical bars on each side of the number:

$$|+5| = +5$$
$$|-5| = +5$$
$$|\ 0| = \ \ 0$$

absolute zero. In science, this is the total absence of heat, the temperature at which all thermal motion in matter stops. Theoretically it would be 273° below zero *Celsius* or 459° below zero *Fahrenheit*.

abstract. To single out an item or idea for emphasis, abridge;

in *set theory,* to single out a particular property which two or more sets, or the elements in one set, have in common.

abstract algebra. A type of algebra consisting of a *set* of *elements, operations* on these elements, and a set of *axioms* or *postulates.* From these, various propositions can be derived.

abstraction. The process of identifying common *properties.* Thus, whole number as a concept is based upon abstracting the common properties of *sets* of *elements.* For example, the legs of a bridge table and a string quartet have the common element of "fourness." From sets like these, we can abstract the idea of the number 4.

abstract number. A number itself, without reference to any particular object or *set* of *elements. Numerals* are the written representations of abstract numbers.

abundant number or excessive number. A *positive integer* whose *factors* (except the integer itself) add up to more than the integer.

acceleration. The rate .of change in *velocity* with respect to time.

account. A bookkeeping record of expenses and payments.

accuracy. See *measured length.*

Achilles (a-KILL-eez) **and the tortoise.** One of the *paradoxes* of *Zeno.* It states that if a tortoise has a headstart on Achilles, a Greek hero, even though Achilles runs faster he can never catch up to the tortoise in a race. While Achilles is making up the headstart, the tortoise goes ahead a little distance; while Achilles makes up the little distance, the tortoise goes another little distance, and so on. The paradox was not solved mathematically until the nineteenth century.

acre. A measurement of land in the United States and Great Britain, equal to 43,560 square feet, 4,840 square yards, or $\frac{1}{640}$ of a square mile.

actual value. The number for which a *numeral* stands.

actuary. A person who uses the branches of mathematics known as *probability* and *statistics* to set insurance rates.

acute angle. An angle whose measure is greater than 0° but less than 90°.

acute triangle. A triangle in which all three angles are acute.

addend. One of a set of numbers to be added. In $4 + 6 = 10$, 4 and 6 are addends and 10 is the *sum.*

adding machine. See *calculating machine.*

addition. A *binary operation* that pairs a number, the *sum,* with two other numbers, the *addends.* The symbol showing that elements are to be added is a + (plus) sign. To find the sum of two numbers such as 2 and 3, we may select two *disjoint sets* with separate or *discrete* elements:

$$A = \{a,b\} \quad B = \{c,d,e\}$$

One set has two elements, the other three. If set A = {a, b} and set B = {c, d, e}, their *union* consists of {a, b, c, d, e}:

$$A \cup B = \{a, b, c, d, e\}$$

**A ∪ B MEANS
"THE UNION
OF SET A AND SET B
CONTAINS a, b, c, d, e."**

There are two elements in set A and three in set B; the number of elements in the union of sets A and B is five. The sum of 2 and 3 is 5.

addition on the number line. Adding numbers on the *number line*.

addition property of equality. For all *real numbers* a, b, and c, if $a = b$, then $a + c = b + c$. See *equality*.

addition property of inequalities. For all *real numbers* a, b, and c, if $a < b$, then $a + c < b + c$. See *inequality*.

additive identity. In addition, the additive identity is zero. The sum of zero and any other number is the number itself.

$$a + 0 = 0 + a = a$$

See *commutative property*.

additive inverse.

$$a + (-a) = (-a) + a = 0$$

For every *integer* there is another integer that, when added to it, gives a sum of zero. Either integer is called the additive inverse of the other. Zero has itself as its additive inverse: $0 + 0 = 0$.

address. The position of any *point* on a *plane*. See *abscissa, ordinate*. In a computer, the position of the tiny magnetic cores that store data.

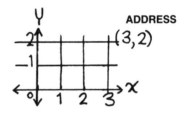

adjacent. Lying next to.

adjacent angles. Two angles in the same *plane* that have a common *vertex* and a common side. They have no interior points in common.

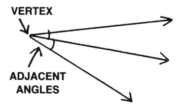

adjacent sides. Sides of a *polygon* that have a common endpoint, or *vertex*. In rectangle ABCD, side AB is adjacent to side BC.

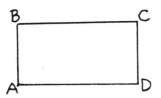

adjoining. Touching, or having a common point, as adjoining triangles.

ADJOINING
TRIANGLES

affine (a-FINE) **geometry.** A kind of geometry in which a figure is projected by *parallel* rays to a plane that can be tilted.

aggregate. The sum or total of a *collection*.

Ahmes (AH-mes) **or Ahmose,** about 1500 B.C. An Egyptian scribe and author of one of the oldest known mathematical texts, written about 3,500 years ago. It contained ways for dealing with fractions and algebraic equations and explained how the circumference of a circle can be divided a fixed number of times by its diameter.

aleph null (AH-leff NULL). The set of natural numbers 1, 2, 3 . . . goes on without end, so we say it is *infinite*. Any set of numbers that can be matched *one-to-one* with the natural numbers is said to have the *cardinal number* aleph null, which is written $\aleph_0$. The set of *common fractions* has the cardinal number aleph null. So does the set of

IN AFFINE GEOMETRY, THE RATIO BETWEEN
THE COLLINEAR POINTS DOES NOT CHANGE.

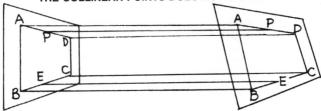

all the even numbers and the set of all the odd numbers. *Georg Cantor,* who invented the arithmetic of infinities, made up the term aleph null using the first letter of the Hebrew alphabet, aleph, $\aleph$ and the Latin word for "none."

Alexandrian School. Another name for the Museum at Alexandria, founded about 300 B.C., which was the ancient world's center of learning for a thousand years. It was the first scientific institution supported by a government, and the most learned scientists studied and taught there. *Euclid* founded the school of mathematics at Alexandria.

algebra. The study of mathematical structure. Elementary algebra is the study of number systems and their *properties.* Algebra solves problems in arithmetic by using letters or symbols to stand for quantities. Algebra is necessary for the study of *calculus, logic, number theory, equation theory, function theory* or combinations of these.

algebraic expression. An expression used in algebra; for example, the following:

a. a *numeral:* 3, .01, ¼, 10^3
b. a *variable:* a, x, y
c. the sum of any two *expressions:* $a + b$, $x + 8$
d. the difference of any two expressions: $x - y$, $14 - z$
e. the *product* of any two expressions: 8y, ab, x^2, $7(m + n)$
f. the *quotient* of any two expressions:

$$\frac{y^2}{x}, \frac{(a + 5)}{-2}$$

See *polynomial, monomial.*

algebraic number. A number that can be produced by addition, subtraction, multiplication, division, or *extracting* a *root* a *finite* number of times.

algorithm (AL-go-rhythm) or algorism. A systematic procedure for carrying out a computation; any method of computing; a step-by-step finite procedure.

Al Khowarizmi (AL CO-war-REEZ-me). A famous Arab algebraist who lived in the ninth century A.D. The word *algorithm* is taken from his name.

alpha. The first letter of the Greek alphabet; α is its symbol. The Greeks gave it a numerical value of 1.

alphanumeric. Computer information that is made up of letters and digits.

alternate exterior angles. In geometry, the relationship of certain angles formed when two or more lines, usually parallel to each other, are *intersected* by a *transversal*. Angles 2 and 7, 1 and 8 are alternate exterior angles.

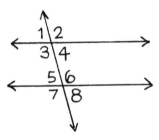

alternate interior angles. In the picture, angles 3 and 6 and 4 and 5 are alternate interior angles.

altimeter (al-TIM-eh-ter). An instrument for showing altitude or distance above land or the sea.

altitude. A *line segment* whose one *endpoint* is the *vertex* of a *polygon* and whose other

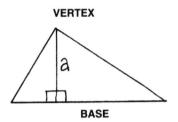

endpoint *intersects* the side opposite the vertex, called the *base*. The altitude is *perpendicular* to the base. The letters a or h are used to denote the altitude or height of a polygon. Every triangle has three altitudes. The altitude of a

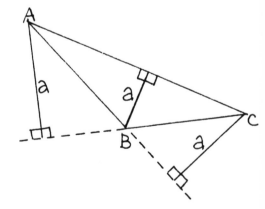

parallelogram is a line segment from any point on the opposite side perpendicular to a line containing the base (any side may be called a base).

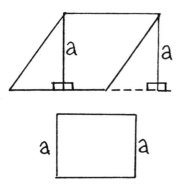

Other figures also have altitudes. The term "altitude" is sometimes used to mean the line segment and also its length.

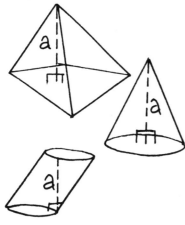

Altitude is also the distance above the surface of the earth. See *table of formulas, on pp. 240–243.*

ambiguous. Having more than one meaning.

amicable numbers. Two numbers, each of which is equal to the sum of all the *factors* of the other number except the number itself. 220 and 284 are amicable numbers. The factors of 220 are 1, 2, 4, 5, 10, 11, 20, 22, 44, 55, and 110, and the sum is 284. The factors of 284 are 1, 2, 4, 71, and 142; the sum is 220.

ampere. A measure of the rate of flow of electrical charges, named for André Ampere, a French mathematician and physicist.

analog computer (AN-uh-log). See *computer.*

analogy. A form of reasoning in which it is assumed that if things are alike in some respects, they are probably alike in other respects. This is not always true.

analysis. A branch of mathematics using the disciplines of *algebra* and *calculus*. It deals with the infinitely large and the infinitely small. In mathematical thought, it is a process of starting at the conclusion and working backward. See *synthesis*.

analysis situs (SY-tus). The technical name for *topology*.

analytic engine. A device invented about 1853 by Charles Babbage, an English mathematician, to solve mathematical problems. It was never completed because the engineering methods of the time were not advanced enough, but it was an important step toward modern computers.

analytic geometry. Also called *Cartesian geometry*. The combining of geometry and algebra to name *points* on a *plane* with reference to a horizontal and a vertical axis.

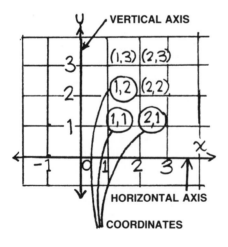

Points are named by *ordered pairs* called *coordinates;* graphs are drawn and curves are studied by means of *equations* and algebraic methods. Analytic geomtery was developed by *René Descartes*. See also *abscissa, ordinate, x-axis, y-axis*.

Anaxagoras (an-axe-a-GOR-as), 500?–428 B.C. A philosopher-mathematician from Smyrna who did most of his work in Greece. While in prison (for saying that the sun was larger than Greece), he worked on *squaring the circle*. He is chiefly known for his discoveries in astronomy.

and. A mathematical *connective*. A *compound sentence*, made up of two *simple sentences*, may be formed by using the word "and." If both simple sentences are true, the compound sentence is true. The symbol for "and" is $\wedge$. For example, $y<5 \wedge 3<y$ means that y is less than 5 and 3 is less than y. If y is 4, both simple sentences are true, since 4 is less than 5 and 3 is less than 4. 4 *satisfies* the connective $y<5 \wedge 3<y$.

The connective "and," when used as an *operation* on

sets, means the *intersection* of two or more sets.

MEANS

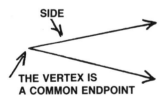

**THE INTERSECTION
OF THESE SETS**

angle. A geometric figure formed by two lines that intersect. The symbol for angle is $\angle$. An angle is also described as the *union* of two *rays* having a common *endpoint.* The two rays are called the *sides* of the angle and the

SIDE

**THE VERTEX IS
A COMMON ENDPOINT**

common endpoint is the *vertex.* See also: *acute angle; adjacent angles; bisector* of an angle; *central angle; corresponding angles; elevation,*

angle of; exterior angle; interior angle; obtuse angle; right angle; straight angle.

angstrom. A unit of length typically used to express atomic distances. 10 angstroms equal 1 *nanometer:* 1nm = 10Å. An angstrom is equal to 0.00000001 centimeter. 10,000,000 angstroms equal 0.001 meter, or 0.04 inch. Å stands for angstrom.

annual. Once a year.

annular. Ring-shaped.

annulus (AN-yuh-lus). The portion of the plane between two concentric circles, one of which is in the interior of the other.

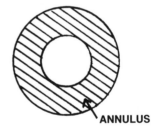

ANNULUS

antecedent. The first *term* of a *ratio.* In ratio 3:4, 3 is the antecedent, 4 is the consequent.

In geometry, the first sentence of a *hypothesis.*

In logic, the sentence that is expressed by the "if" clause. If $2+2=4$, then $2+3=5$. In this sentence, $2+2=4$ is the antecedent.

antilogarithm. The antilogarithm of a given number is the number that has the given number as its *logarithm*. If $\log 3.42 = .5430$, then antilog $.5430 = 3.42$. See *table, pp. 253–254.*

antipodal (an-TIP-o-dal) **points.** The endpoints of a diameter of a sphere.

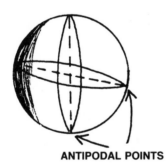

ANTIPODAL POINTS

apex. The highest point relative to some line or plane.

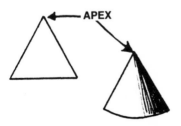

APEX

apogee (AP-o-gee). The most distant or highest point, usually of an orbit.

Apollonius (ap-o-LON-i-us), 260–200 B.C. A Greek geometer whose work so completely detailed what was then known that little was added to it for 1,500 years. He is chiefly known for his work with *conic sections*. He was also a fine arithmetician and astronomer.

apothecaries' (a-POTH-uh-carries) **fluid measure.** The liquid measure used in making drugs or prescriptions. See *table, p. 246.*

apothecaries' weight. The standard weights and measures used for drugs. (Pharmacists also use the metric system.) See *table, p. 244.*

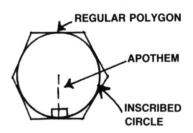

REGULAR POLYGON
APOTHEM
INSCRIBED CIRCLE

apothem (AP-o-them). A *radius* (or length of radius) of the *inscribed circle* of a *reg-*

ular polygon, drawn perpendicular to a side of the polygon.

applied mathematics. Mathematics put to practical use, as in physics, mechanics, or surveying, among others. When the concepts of space and number are joined with time, matter, magnetism, even relativity, it is considered applied mathematics.

approximation. see *estimation.*

Arabic numerals. The Hindu-Arabic numeration system, used most commonly today: 0, 1, 2, 3, 4, 5, 6, 7, 8, 9.

Arabs, mathematics of. From about the ninth to the fifteenth centuries A.D., the Arabs translated and kept alive the earlier Greek and Hindu writings that were later retranslated into Latin and English. Arab contributions were mainly in arithmetic and algebra.

arbitrary constant. See *constant.*

arc. A part of a circle. A *subset* of the set of *points* of a circle. In the drawing, points A and B are *endpoints* of mi-

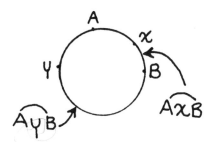

nor arc AxB and major arc AyB. An arc that has the endpoints of a diameter as endpoints is called a semicircle. The symbol for arc is ⌒ .

arc and angle measurement. See *table, pp. 240–241.*

Archimedes (ar-ki-MEE-deez) **of Samos,** 287–212 B.C. One of the great mathematicians of all time. He gave *proofs* for finding the *areas, vol-*

umes, and centers of gravity for *circles, spheres, conics, spirals, curves,* and *surfaces.* He began the sciences of *calculus,* of hydrostatics, and of mechanics. A great inventor, too, he discovered the laws of the lever and pulley. He was one of the first to apply scientific thinking to everyday problems.

arcs. In *topology,* the lines on a network. In Euler's *Königsberg Bridge problem,* each arc represented a bridge.

NETWORK

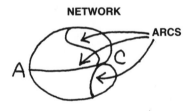

Arctic Circle. An imaginary circle on the earth, parallel to the equator. It is approximately 23°27′ from the North Pole.

are. A metric unit of area, 100 square meters; 119.6 square yards.

area. The amount of surface. The measure of a *closed re-*

gion of a *plane* is called its area. A standard unit of area is the square inch. There are formulas for finding the areas of many kinds of figures. See *table of formulas, pp. 240–241.* See *volume* for three dimensional figures.

area measure, surveyor's. The system of measurement used by surveyors. See *table, p. 246.*

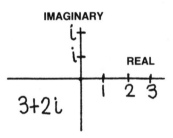

Argand diagram. A diagram that provides a frame of reference for graphing complex numbers. The horizontal axis is for the real part; the vertical axis for the imaginary part.

argument of a function. The independent *variable.*

Aristarchus (AR-is-TAR-kus) **of Samos,** 3rd century B.C. Greek mathematician who was the first to work out the length of the year. He tried to calculate the distance from the earth to the moon and the sun and concluded that the distance from the earth to the sun is some twenty times the distance from that of the earth to the moon.

Aristotle (AR-is-tot-l), 384–322 B.C. A Greek philosopher who laid the foundations for most of the branches of science and philosophy known today. He had great influence on Western thinking, especially as a philosopher, political thinker, and biologist.

arithmetic. The branch of mathematics concerned with the rules for operations on numbers.

arithmetic, fundamental theorem. Any *positive integer* can be *factored* into *primes* in only one way, apart from the order in which the prime factors are written. This is also called the *unique factorization theorem.*

arithmetica (ar-rith-MEH-ti-ca). The study of numbers, especially in ancient times, to find various interesting relationships between them.

arithmetic laws. There are eleven properties or laws for arithmetic:

The *closure property for addition.*

The *closure property for multiplication.*

The *commutative property for addition.*

The *commutative property for multiplication.*

The *identity property for addition.*

The *identity property for multiplication.*

The *associative property for addition.*

The *associative property for multiplication.*

The *inverse property for addition.*

The *inverse property for multiplication.*

The *distributive property.*

arithmetic mean. The mean, or average, of a set of numbers is found by dividing the sum of the numbers by the number of numbers. See *cen-*

ARITHMETIC MEAN

$$
\begin{array}{r}
5 \\
8 \\
9 \\
6 \\
\hline
28
\end{array}
\qquad
4\overline{)28}^{\,7}
$$

tral tendency. Arithmetic mean or means may also refer to the other *terms* of an *arithmetic progression* of which the first and last terms are specified. The arithmetic mean of 8 and 10 is 9.

arithmetic number. A *subset* of the *real number* system; any real, *nonnegative number.*

arithmetic operation. In common use, the four fundamental operations are *addition, subtraction, multiplication,* and *division.* An operation applied to two *members* of a *set* identifies a third *element* of the set. For example, the operation addition, for 3 and 7, gives 10.

$$\{1,2,3,4,5,6,7,8,9,10...\}$$
$$3+7 \underline{\qquad\qquad} \uparrow$$

arithmetic progression. See *patterning.*

arrangement. A special way of setting out or ordering a collection of things, or the *members* of a *set.* A set of nine things, for example,

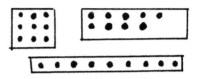

might be arranged in many ways. See *permutation.*

array. An orderly arrangement of objects in rows and columns. An egg carton is an example of a 2-by-6 array.

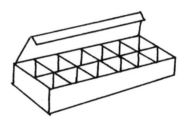

arrow in motion. One of the *paradoxes* of *Zeno,* which stated that, since the arrow is always in a given position at a given time, it is always at rest and never moves. (It is like separate frames in a strip of movie film. Nothing moves in any frame.) How, then, does an object move? The paradox was not answered for almost 2,000 years.

arrows on lines and rays in geometry. Show that the *line* or *ray* extends infinitely in the direction of the arrow.

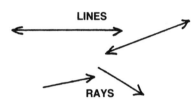

LINES

RAYS

arrows to show one-to-one correspondence. See *mapping, one-to-one correspondence.*

$$\{1, 2, 3, 4, 5\}$$
$$\{a, b, c, d, e\}$$

arrows used as symbols. *Connectives* in logic.

$$P \rightarrow Q$$

ascending. Increasing. In $x^2 + x^3 + x^4$, the exponents are in ascending order.

assessed value. The value assigned to property for the purpose of taxing it. Assessed value is usually only a certain percentage of the current market value.

assets. The financial goods and property, resources of a business.

assigning. Matching or *associating* a number or letter with a point. The points on this line can be assigned numbers like 1, 2, 3, 4, or letters like A, B, C, D.

$$\begin{array}{cccc} 1 & 2 & 3 & 4 \\ A & B & C & D \end{array}$$

associating. Matching or *assigning.*

associative property for addition. The property by which *addends* may be grouped and added in any order, without changing the sum. $(1 + 2) + 3 = 6$. So does $1 + (2 + 3)$. In general, the property for all real numbers may be stated $(a + b) + c = a + (b + c)$.

associative property for multiplication. If any three numbers are multiplied in a given order, the *factors* may be grouped in any way without changing the product. $(2 \times 3) \times 4$ is the same as $2 \times (3 \times 4)$. The product of both is 24. In general, the property for all real numbers is $(ab)c = a(bc)$.

assumptions. A mathematical system depends upon a set of *propositions* which are assumed to be true. From these assumed propositions, other propositions may be deduced. Assumptions, in turn, are used to prove certain *theorems.* See *axiom, postulate.*

astrology. A pseudoscience using mathematics and astronomy. It was a failed theory because it was based on a false *model.*

asymptote. A line that approaches another line but never reaches it.

atom. The smallest component of an *element.* An atom is composed of a *nucleus* and the *electrons* moving around it.

atomic number. The number of protons in the *nucleus* of an *atom.* The atomic number determines the place of an *element* in the *periodic table* (see *250–251*) of elements.

EIGHT PROTONS GIVE AN OXYGEN ATOM THE ATOMIC NUMBER 8

ITS ATOMIC WEIGHT IS 16

atomic weight. The weight of an atom, compared with the weight of an atom of oxygen, which is set at 16 atomic mass units. Atomic weight is usually about the same as the total number of protons and neutrons in its nucleus, which is called the mass number.

Atwood, George, 1746–1807. An English mathematician who wrote many books on mathematics. He invented Atwood's machine, which was used in the study of falling bodies, showing the relation of time, speed, and motion under the force of graviation.

automation. The use of computers combined with robots to perform work.

average. A single number representing a set of numbers. See *arithmetic mean*. It is one measure of *central tendency*. To find an average, see *table of formulas, p. 243*.

average deviation. A measure used in *statistics* that shows how the *data* is grouped or spread about the measure of *central tendency*.

avoirdupois (av-er-du-POIZ) **weight.** A system of weights used in the United States and Great Britain for all commodities except drugs, jewels, and precious metals. See *table, p. 244*.

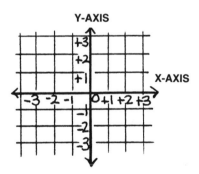

axes, (AX-eez) **coordinate.** The *x-axis* and the *y-axis*, used to locate *Cartesian coordinates*. See *abscissa, origin, axis, analytic geometry*.

axial. Pertaining to an axis, or line.

axiom. Imagine mathematics as a set of statements. We accept certain statements to be true. From these first statements, other statements are then proved. The assumed statements are called axioms, *assumptions,* or *postulates.* The geometry of *Euclid* was based on certain axioms which, centuries later, were recognized to be assumptions and not "self-evident truths." Whole new geometries were invented by accepting different sets of axioms.

axis. The *number line* of a *graph* is called the *coordinate axis.* The horizontal number line is called the *x-axis.* The vertical number line is called the *y-axis.* Their point of intersection is called the *origin.*

Some geometric figures have axes. The axis of a *cone* is a *line segment* from the center of the *base* to the *vertex.*

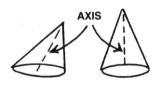

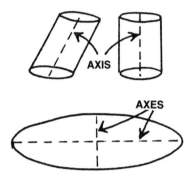

The axis of a *cylinder* is the *line segment* joining the center of the two *bases*. An *ellipse* has two axes.

axis of a parabola. A line about which both parts of a parabola are symmetrical.

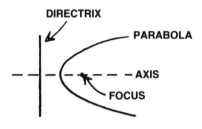

axis of symmetry. The line about which a geometrical figure is symmetrical, such as the altitude of an equilateral triangle or the diameter of a circle. Imagine a drawing folded along the axis. Every point on one half of the figure would fall on a point on the other side.

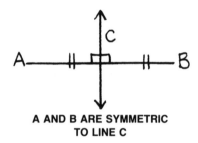

A AND B ARE SYMMETRIC TO LINE C

Two points are symmetric with respect to a line if the line is the *perpendicular bisector* of the line segment of which the points are the endpoints.

B

B. The capital letter B is used to name a *point;*

an *angle;*

the *vertex* of a *polygon;*

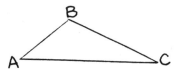

a *set* of *elements:*
B = {6, 7, 8, 9};

B is used in *formulas;*

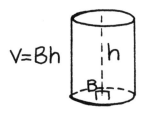

as the abbreviation for *base.*

b. The lowercase letter b is used as a *variable* in a *formula* and to represent the measure of a side of a *polygon.*

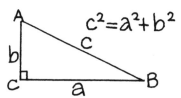

It is used to name a *line.*

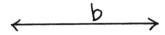

It is used in *equations,* as a *variable.* 3b = 27.

It is also used to express general *properties.* For example, since the order of multiplying two numbers does not change the product, the property may be stated a × b = b × a.

Babbage, Charles, 1792–1871. An English mathematician, engineer, and inventor. He invented and solved codes of all kinds, devised a system of identifying lighthouses by the pattern of their beams, and invented the first speedometer. He designed a *difference engine* for calculating logarithms to twenty decimal places and an *analytic engine* that was, in theory, much like today's computers. Babbage's ideas were

60 is still the basis for our time system: 60 seconds = 1 minute; 60 minutes = 1 hour. Measurements in astronomy are based on 60, too.

so far beyond the engineering techniques of his time that neither machine could be successfully completed.

Babylonian numeration system. A *numeration system* used in ancient times, with a *base* of 60. The Babylonians wrote on clay and their numerals were wedge-shaped. Their system looked like this:

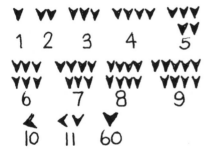

Bacon, Roger, 1214–1294. An English scientist whose ideas were so advanced that he was accused of magic. He said that mathematics was the alphabet of philosophy. He showed how astronomy and the other physical sciences rest on mathematics, and how it is only when their principles are stated in mathematical form that they progress.

balance. An equal distribution. Also, the amount owed on an article after a down payment has been made. Finally, a scale for weighing.

balance, bank. The amount of money in a bank account.

balance sheet. In bookkeeping, a listing of assets on the left side of the sheet and liabilities on the right side of the sheet. The sums of the two columns should balance.

ball. A *spherical* object.

ballistics. The study of the motion of projectiles, such as bullets or missiles.

bank discount. The money taken by the bank as interest on a loan and deducted from the face value of the loan.

bank statement. A record of a checking account, usually issued monthly to a depositor.

bar. The *line segment* used in a fraction to separate the numerator from the denominator. Also called a *vinculum*.

$$\frac{3}{4} \quad \longleftarrow \text{BAR}$$

bar graph. See *graph*.

base as a factor. The number, symbol, or *variable* used with an *exponent*. In 6^4, 6 is the base. 6^4 means $6 \times 6 \times 6 \times 6$. The base is the number used as a *factor*.

base eight system. A numeration system in which objects are grouped by eights. Also called the *octal system*.

base in percent. To find 30% of $47, 47 is the base, which is multiplied by the rate, .30. A formula that is often used is $p = br$. The b is the base number and the r is the percent number. See *table, p. 243*.

base of a geometric figure. In the triangle below, the side opposite the vertex angle A is called the base of the triangle.

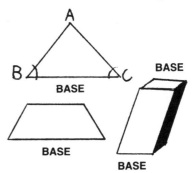

The angles B and C are called the base angles. Many geometric figures have sides or portions of planes as their bases.

base of a numeration system. The number on which a numeration system is constructed. In our base ten system, 234 means two hundreds + three tens + four ones.

PLACE VALUE CHART, BASE TEN		
HUNDREDS	TENS	ONES
2	3	4

base sixteen system. Also called hexadecimal system. Most computers now use base sixteen or even base thirty-two for their operations.

base ten system. See *decimal system.*

base two system. See *binary system.*

basic fraction. The simplest *fraction,* for example, ¾.
 A fraction in which the numerator and denominator have no *common factor* other than 1 and −1.

basic pair. An *ordered pair* of *rational numbers* in which one member of the pair is zero.

basic table. Any operational table in arithmetic. It is made up of a grid of straight lines that form squares. The numerals in the squares show the results of the operations for which each table is designed.

BASE ADDITION TABLE TO 3 + 3 = 6. WHERE THE LINES INTERSECT, IS THE SUM OR ANSWER, 3 + 2 = 5.

+	1	2	3
1	2	3	4
2	3	4	5
3	4	5	6

bel. A unit of sound named for Alexander Graham Bell. Equal to 10 *decibels.*

bell-shaped curve. The normal curve of *distribution.*

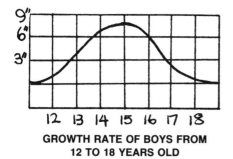

**GROWTH RATE OF BOYS FROM
12 TO 18 YEARS OLD**

Notice that the greatest *frequency* occurs in the middle with a tapering off at each end.

Beltrami, Eugenio, 1835–1900. Italian mathematician, famous for his work on *non-Euclidean geometry,* electricity, and magnetism. He was the inventor of the *pseudosphere,* on which the geometry of *Lobachevski* is based.

beneficiary. The person named by the owner of a life insurance policy as the one to whom the value of the policy should be paid when the insured dies.

Bernoulli (ber-NOO-lee) **or Bernouilli.** A Swiss family that, from 1654 to 1782, produced eight great mathematicians. The most famous were the versatile brothers Jakob and Johann, both teachers. They were among the first to understand the importance of *differential* and *integral calculus,* and they established fundamental principles in *probability.* Daniel, the son of Johann, won ten prizes from the French Academy of Sciences.

beta. The second letter of the Greek alphabet and the Greek name for the numeral 2. The symbol for beta is β.

between. Refers to an *interval* that does not include the first and last *elements.* For example, "The set of whole numbers between 3 and 7," would mean the numbers 4, 5, and 6.

betweenness. See *density.*

Bhaskara (BUS-kah-rah), 1114–1185. A Hindu mathematician who wrote the *Lilāvati* (named for his daughter) and several other important books on mathematics. He developed the following rules related to zero, which he called "cipher."

1. If cipher is added to a number, the sum is the same as the number.

2. If cipher is subtracted from a number, the result is still the number itself.

3. If a number is multiplied by cipher, the result is cipher.

He also introduced the idea of *negative numbers* and of the *additive inverse*.

bi. A prefix meaning "two" or "twice," as in bilateral, biangular, or binary.

biconditional. In a *compound sentence*, if the *connective* is in the form of "if and only if," the statement is called biconditional. The symbol for biconditional is written $\longleftrightarrow$ OR $\Longleftrightarrow$

billion. A thousand million in the United States; a million million in Great Britain.

binary (BY-na-ree) **operation.** An operation performed on two *elements* at a time. Addition and multiplication are both binary operations. For example, you can add $23 + 64$, and you can multiply 23 and 64.

binary system. A numeration system that uses only two numerals, usually 0 and 1, to express all numbers. 0 and 1 can also indicate the positions of off and on. Only the use of *place value* makes this possible. Computers all originally used the binary system, sometimes called dyadic notation.

binomial (by-NOME-ee-al). A binomial is the algebraic *sum* of two *monomials*. Some examples of binomials are: $2 + 3$, $x + 1$, $2x - 1$, $3x - 4y$, $m^2 - 2m$. See *polynomial*.

binomial (by-NOME-ee-al) **distribution.** A *distribution* of a number of successes in a series of trials where each trial can end in either success or failure. Counting the number of times a tossed coin turns up heads or tails is this kind of trial.

binomial theorem. A rule for writing out an *equivalent* expansion of an expression such as $(a + b)^2$ without having to perform all the multiplication involved. The answer, in this case $a^2 + 2ab + b^2$, was first shown by *Omar Khayyam*, then by *Descartes* and *Newton*. In the binomial theorem, the *coefficient* of the first and last terms is 1, and the coef-

PLACE VALUE CHART BASE TWO (BINARY SYSTEM).				
EIGHTS $(2 \times 2 \times 2)$	**FOURS** (2×2)	**TWOS** (2)	**ONES**	**NUMBERS**
			0	← 0
			1	← 1
		1	0	← 2
		1	1	← 3
	1	0	0	← 4
	1	0	1	← 5

IN THE BINARY SYSTEM,   5 IS 101, BASE TWO
                               8 IS 1000, BASE TWO
                        15 IS 1111, BASE TWO

ficient of the second and next-to-last terms is the same as the *exponent*. The number of terms written out is one more than the exponent. For example, $(a + b)^5$ is $a^5 + 5a^4b + 10a^3b^2 + 10a^2b^3 + 5ab^4 + b^5$.

biometry (by-OHM-eh-tree). The application of mathematics, especially *statistics*, to the study and measurement of living things.

bisect. To cut or divide into two equal parts.

bisector. In geometry, a straight *line segment* that divides another line segment, or an angle, into two congruent parts.

BISECTOR

bit. The shortened term for binary digit, either I or O. IOIO is a four-bit number.

body of a matrix. The part of a table that shows the results of the operation. See *matrix*.

Boethius (bo-EE-the-us), A.D. 475–525. A Roman philosopher who translated the works of the ancient mathematicians and bridged the gap between the knowledge of the Greeks and that of the Middle Ages.

Bohr, Niels (BORE), 1885–1962. Danish physicist who proposed the structure of the atom in which electrons revolve around the nucleus in orbits, or shells, at specific distances, and each shell contains a specific number of electrons.

Bolyai, Johann (BOL-yai, YO-hahn), 1802–1860. Hungarian mathematician who at the age of twenty-two wrote *The Absolute Science of Space,* a complete system of geometry. He showed that *Euclid's parallel postulate* was not necessary and that a whole system of geometry could be based on the *pseudosphere* of *Beltrami.* Although he was one

of the founders of *non-Euclidean geometry,* he had been preceded (unknown to him) by *Gauss* and *Lobachevksi.*

Bolyai, Wolfgang (BOL-yai, VOLF-gang), 1775–1856. Father of *Johann Bolyai.* He studied with *Gauss* and tried to prove *Euclid's parallel postulate.*

bookkeeping. The work of keeping the account books and records of a business firm.

Boolean algebra. The beginning of the algebra of logic, formulated in 1847 by George Boole. It has two main divisions: the algebra of *classes* and the algebra of relations. Boole is also credited with formulating *axioms* in the algebra of *sets.*

Boole, George (BOOL), 1815–1864. An Englishman who helped develop modern symbolic *logic.* He was one of the first mathematicians to realize that *symbols* of *operation* could be separated from those of *quantity.* He showed that classes or sets of objects could be operated on in the same way algebraic symbols or numerical quantities can.

Boole applied ordinary algebra to the logic of *classes*. One of the many modern applications of Boolean algebra is its use in the design of computers. Boole also applied his laws of reasoning to the mathematics of *probability* and produced a view of an abstract *calculus*.

borrowing. A term used in subtraction. In more recent times, a number is said to be *renamed* and then the subtraction process carried out.

$$64 = 60 + 4 = 50 + 14$$
$$-39 = 30 + 9 = 30 + 9$$
$$20 + 5 = 25$$

64 is renamed 50 + 14.

boundary. A boundary can be:

1. A *point* that separates a *line* into two *half-lines*.

BOUNDARY

2. A line that separates a *plane* into two *half-planes*.

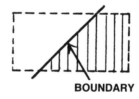

BOUNDARY

3. A plane that separates *space* into two *half-spaces*.
4. The set of points of a closed figure that separates a plane into two *regions*.

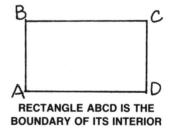

**RECTANGLE ABCD IS THE
BOUNDARY OF ITS INTERIOR**

A boundary separates a plane into three sets of points: the

interior set, the exterior set, and the set that makes up the boundary.

braces. Used in *set notation* to identify the *elements* of a set. The braces also stand for the word "set" when reading or writing about sets.

$$A = \{1, 2, 3\}$$

The set A contains members 1, 2, and 3.

brackets. Brackets, like parentheses, indicate that the quantities enclosed are to be treated as a unit.

$$2 \times [6 - (2 \times 2)] = 4.$$

Brahe, Tycho (BRAH-eh, TIE-ko), 1546–1601. A Scandinavian mathematician and as-

tronomer who collected the most accurate and greatest number of astronomical facts prior to the invention of the telescope. He left his table of planetary motions for *Kepler* to finish. The imperial mathematician to Emperor Rudolph II, Brahe is said to have lost the tip of his nose in a duel over a geometry problem. He discovered and measured the position of a brilliant supernova, now called Tycho's star. His name was also given to one of the craters of the moon. In his theory of the universe, the earth was the center.

Briggs, Henry (or Harry), 1561–1630. An English professor of geometry who recognized the importance of the *logarithms* of *Napier* and originated the work that led to the use of 10 as the base for the tables of logarithms. See *tables, pp. 253–254.*

broken line. A union of *line segments* joined end to end but not in a straight line. No more than two segments can have a common *endpoint*.

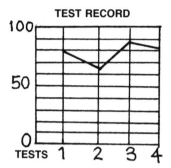

TEST RECORD

broken-line graph. A diagram showing how an *ordered pair* of items are related by connecting points on a grid with line segments.

Brouwer, Luityen (BROW-er, LIGHT-ain), 1881–? A Dutch mathematician who made great contributions to *topology* and the theory of *sets*. Brouwerian mathematics states that intuition can help to solve mathematical problems.

Brownian motion. The irregular motion of small particles in a gas or liquid when bombarded by molecules.

Buffon needle problem. An experiment in *probability* by the Comte de Buffon, an eighteenth-century French mathematician. He showed that if a needle is dropped on a flat surface that has parallel lines on it, the number of times the needle falls across a line closely approximates the value of *pi (π)*. The parallel lines are set a distance apart. The length of the needle is such that $1 < d$. The probability that the needle will intersect one of the lines is $p = 2 \ 1/\pi d$.

THE NEEDLE MUST BE SHORTER THAN THE DISTANCE BETWEEN THE LINES

bushel. A unit of *dry measure,* containing 4 *pecks.* See *table, p. 246.*

Bush, Vannevar, 1890–1974. American engineer, mathematician, and physicist who, in 1931, built the first large modern analog *computer.* He coordinated the scientific research on the atomic bomb project and was director of the U.S. Office of Scientific Research and Development during World War II.

byte (BITE). A group of eight binary digits, or *bits,* which can represent a letter, a number, or a punctuation mark.

C

C. The capital letter is used to name a *point;*

.C

an *angle;*

the *vertex* of a *polygon;*

a *set* of *elements:*

C = {8, 9, 10}

in *formulas;*

$$C = 2\pi r$$

the Roman numeral for 100.

C is also the abbreviation for Celsius and for *circumference.*

c. The lowercase letter is used as a *variable* in a *formula;*

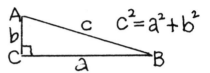

$$c^2 = a^2 + b^2$$

to represent the measure of the side of a *polygon;*

to name a *line;*

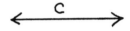

in *equations,* as a *variable.*
3c = 9;

to express general *properties.*
a(bc) = a(cb).

c is the abbreviation for the speed of light.

calculating machines. Devices that solve problems in arithmetic: addition, subtraction, multiplication, and division. All calculating machines were developed from the adding machine, which is the simplest. *Computers* are complex calculating machines. See also *calculator; Pascal.*

calculation. The act of computing or figuring.

calculate. To get a result by carrying out a mathematical process.

calculator. A hand-held electronic device that has replaced mathematical tables and slide rules. Usually battery operated, it is inexpensive and an important tool for math students.

calculus. Calculus was discovered in the seventeenth century, independently by *Isaac Newton* of England and *Gottfried Leibniz* of Germany. It is a field of mathematics with tremendous applications to physics, chemistry, engineering, biology, economics, and many other areas. Basic to calculus is the idea of *limit*. Calculus deals with changing quantities and with motion. In *differential calculus,* the idea of limit allows us to find the instantaneous rate of change (called the derivative) of a *function. Integral calculus* is used to find the work done by a force, and to solve geometric problems. *Archimedes* was one of the first to use a kind of calculus.

calendar. A method of measuring and recording time, especially in cycles of a year, including the arrangement of days into weeks and of weeks into months. Most calendars are based on the solar year, the time it takes the earth to make one complete orbit around the sun. Some calendars are based on the lunar month, the period from one new moon to the next.

calibration. The marking off of an instrument into units for measuring.

calipers. Instruments for measuring dimensions, the thickness or diameter of an object, or the distance between surfaces. Some calipers are a graduated rule with one sliding part and one fixed part. Some have two legs, usually curved.

cancel. To add equal quantities to both *members* of an *equation;* to divide out a *factor* common to both *terms* of a *fraction.*

candle power. The standard measure of light set by international agreement. The brightness of electric lights is measured in candle power.

Cantor, Georg, 1845–1918. A German mathematician born

in St. Petersburg, Russia. He taught at the University of Halle from 1869–1913. He is known for his work on the theory of numbers, particularly infinite classes. He introduced the term "transfinite numbers" and the symbols to represent them, starting with *aleph null*.

cap. The symbol for *intersection* of *sets*. A ∩ B is read, "A cap B," or "the intersection of A and B."

capacity. The number of *cubic units* a container can hold, which is called the *volume* of the container.

Cardano (called **Cardan**), **Girolamo,** 1501–1576. An Italian mathematician who, by a ruse, forced *Tartaglia* to teach him his method of solving a *cubic equation,* which he published as his own. Although it was later proved to be Tartaglia's, the solution is still known as "Cardan's solution of the cubic." Cardano also recognized the importance of negative *roots*.

cardinality of a set. The number of *elements* in a *set,* without regard to the kinds of elements. If set R = {a, b, 3, 5}, then the *cardinal number* of set R is 4.

cardinal number. A number that describes how many are in a *set* of things. Two sets have the same cardinal number if the *elements* in the sets can be matched one-to-one. Each of the following sets has the cardinal number 2.

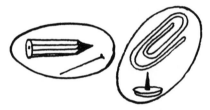

cardioid (KAR-dee-oid). If one circle is stationary and a second circle of equal size rolls around it, the path made by a point on the moving circle is called a cardioid.

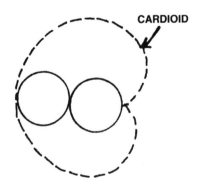

CARDIOID

caret (KAR-et). A mark, ∧, often used in division, when the decimal points in the *divisor* and in the *dividend* are both "moved" the same number of places to the right.

To express numbers in *scientific notation,* for example, in 93000000, a caret is placed after the first *significant digit:* 9 ∧ 3000000. This helps us find the *exponent.*

$$9_{\wedge}3000000 = 9.3 \times 10^7.$$

Carroll, Lewis. 1832–1898. The pseudonym of Charles Lutwidge Dodgson, English writer and mathematician. He lectured in mathematics at Oxford, wrote on *Euclid,* and invented many mathematical brainteasers. His mathematical writing is often forgotten in favor of his famous book *Alice in Wonderland.*

carrying. A *computational* process used in addition when the sum of a column is as great or greater than the *base* used. For example, in our base ten system, whenever the sum of a single column is more than 9, the last *digit* of the sum is written under that column and the remaining figures are added to the *addends* of the next column to the left. Carrying is now often called *regrouping.* For example, fourteen 1's are regrouped as one 10 and four 1's.

Cartesian (car-TEE-zhun) **coordinates.** Every point in a *plane* is given an *address.* This address is an ordered pair of numbers, the first of which is called the *abscissa.* The numbers associated with the point are called the *coordinates* of the point.

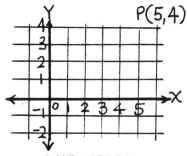

5 AND 4 ARE THE
COORDINATES OF P

Cartesian geometry. Usually called *analytic geometry.* *René Descartes* and *Pierre de Fermat* worked independently on it. Basically it is the joining of geometry and algebra. A correspondence is developed so that curves can

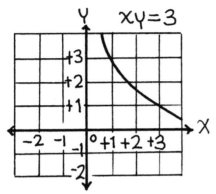

be studied in terms of their *equations*.

Cartesian set or product. The *set* of all *ordered pairs,* made by matching every element in the first set with every element in the second set. If the first set, A, consists of the numbers 1 and 2, and the second set, B, consists of the numbers 3, 4, and 5, then the Cartesian product or set, A × B, consists of (1, 3), (1, 4), (1, 5), (2, 3), (2, 4), and (2, 5). See *cross*. The members of A are the first *components* of the ordered pairs, and the members of B are the second components of the ordered pairs. Notice that in set A there are two elements, in set B there are three elements, and in their Cartesian product there are six elements.

catenary. The curve formed by a string or chain hanging from two fixed points.

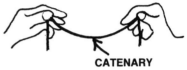

CATENARY

Cauchy (KOH-shee) **Augustin Louis,** 1789–1857. French mathematician who was a professor at three colleges in Paris at the same time. His work was influential in every branch of mathematics, especially in *calculus,* the theory of functions, and algebraic *analysis*. He published almost eight hundred writings.

Cavalieri (kav-al-YEAH-ri), **Francesco,** 1598–1647. Italian mathematician and Jesuit priest who taught at Bologna. He invented the method of indivisibles, which was the forerunner of integral calculus. Cavalieri's theorem is concerned with solids of equal volume.

Cayley, Arthur, 1821–1895. English mathematician who taught at Cambridge. He worked in pure mathematics, especially the theory of *matrices* and the theory of *invariants*.

cc. Abbreviation for *cubic centimeter*.

Celsius (SELL-see-us). The metric system temperature scale first proposed by Swedish astronomer Anders Celsius. See *centigrade*.

cent. A penny, the hundredth part of a U.S. dollar.

center. In a circle, the *point* in the *plane* that is equidistant from all points on the *circle*. A *line segment* from the center to the circle is called a *radius*. Radii of a circle are all equal in length.

center of a sphere. A *point* equally distant from all points on the *sphere*.

centesimal (sen-TES-i-mal). Division into a hundred equal parts, usually referring to a system of measuring angles. In the centesimal system a *right angle* is divided into 100 parts or degrees; a degree is divided into 100 angular minutes; a minute is divided into 100 angular seconds. In this system, which is not in common use, a circle has 400

centesimal degrees instead of the usual 360 degrees.

centi. A prefix meaning one hundred.

centigrade. The metric system scale for measuring temperature in degrees, now universally referred to as the *Celsius scale,* in honor of the man who proposed it. On this scale the freezing point of water is 0° and the boiling point is 100°.

centigram. $1/100$ of a *gram,* equal to 0.1543 *grain.* See *table, pp. 248–249.*

centiliter. $1/100$ of a *liter,* equal to 0.6102 *cubic inch* or 0.338 U.S. *fluid ounce.* See *table, pp. 248–249.*

centimeter. $1/100$ of a *meter,* equal to 0.3937 inch. See *table, pp. 248–249.*

central angle. An angle with its *vertex* at the center of a circle.

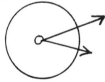

central tendency, measures of. In *statistics,* the terms "mean" (or "average"), "median," and "mode" are ways of indicating the place on a *distribution curve* where the largest number of items are concentrated. If the average mark on an exam is 80, that is the mean. If half the class had a mark above 75, that is the median; if more students had 85 than any other score, that is the mode. These are called measures of central tendency.

century. One hundred years.

cgs system. The *metric system* of measurement in which the three fundamental units are the *centimeter*, the *gram*, and the *second*. See *absolute unit*.

chain measure. A system of measurement used by surveyors. See *table, p. 246*.

chance. See *probability*.

change of base. A numeral such as 13 in *base ten* may be changed to 23 in *base five*.

BASE TEN		BASE FIVE	
TENS	ONES	FIVES	ONES
1	3	2	3

Both numerals represent the same number.

chaos (KAY-os). In mathematics, the study of pattern or order in turbulence and disorder.

characteristic. See *logarithms*.

checking. A method of showing whether or not a solution is correct. The method for checking subtraction is addition. See also *proof*.

$$\begin{array}{cc} 97 & 34 \\ -63 & +63 \\ \hline 34 & 97 \end{array}$$

chevron. The symbol $>$ (is *greater than*) or $<$ (is *less than*). It can be written $\geq$ (is greater than or *equal* to), or $\leq$ (is less than or equal to). The bar changes the meaning.

Chinese, early mathematics of. The early Chinese were fine mathematicians. Almost five thousand years ago they had a numeration system based on two numbers, like the *binary system* used in computers.

chip. A minute package of microscopic electronic circuitry used in computers.

chisambop. A Korean method of using fingers to do arithmetic operations. Multiplication of numbers over 5 is done this way: To multiply 9 by 8, on one hand raise four fingers to represent the difference between 9 and the number of fingers on the hand. On the other hand, raise three fingers to show the difference between the second number (8), and the fingers (5) on that hand. The total number of fingers raised (7) is the number of tens in the product.

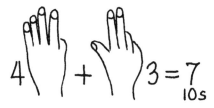

Then the number of closed fingers on one hand (1) is multiplied by the number closed on the other hand (2), to get the number of ones. $1 \times 2 = 2$, $70 + 2 = 72$.

chord. A *line segment* whose endpoints are on the circle. See also *diameter*.

chronology. The science of arranging time in periods and establishing the dates and historical order of past events.

chronometer. A very precise clock, accurate to within a second or two over a period of months. It is used mainly aboard ships to help determine their position at sea.

ciphers. See *codes, numerals, zero*.

circle. A *set* of all *points* in a *plane* at a fixed distance from a fixed point in the plane. The fixed point is called the center or focus of the circle.

A circle divides a plane into three sets of points:

1. The set of all points outside the circle;

2. The set of all points inside the circle; and

3. The set of all points on the circle.

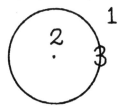

circle, area of. See *table, p. 240.*

circle, great. The *intersection* of a *sphere* and a *plane* that passes through the center of that sphere. It is the shortest distance from one point on a sphere to another.

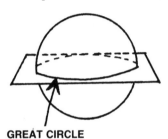

GREAT CIRCLE

circle, small. The *intersection* of a *sphere* and a *plane* that does not pass through the center of the sphere.

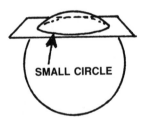

SMALL CIRCLE

circle, squaring the. Squaring the circle is one of the most famous problems in the history of mathematics. Using only a *straightedge* and *compass,* ancient geometers tried to construct a square equal in area to a given circle and found it impossible. To square the circle, a *line segment* of length $\sqrt{\pi}$ must be constructed from a unit line segment. In 1882 it was shown that π and $\sqrt{\pi}$ are not *algebraic.* Any length constructable by straightedge and compass from a unit segment is algebraic; therefore, it is impossible to square the circle in terms of Euclidean geometry.

circle graph. See *graph.*

circular closed region. The *union* of a circle and its *interior.*

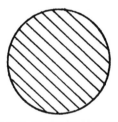

CIRCULAR CLOSED REGION

circular measure. See *table, p. 247.*

circumference. The measure of the distance around a circle. See *table of formulas, p. 240.*

circumscribe. A circumscribed circle is a circle passing through all the *vertices* of a *polygon.*

CLOSED BROKEN LINES

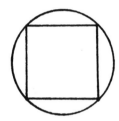

CIRCUMSCRIBED CIRCLE

class. A collection of things. It may be the class of all the whole numbers, the class of all boys named Steve, or the class of stars larger than the sun. The class may be *finite,* like the class of redheaded grocers in a town, or it may be *infinite,* like the class of fractions.

Mathematicians also call a class a *set,* a collection, an aggregate, or a manifold.

clockwise. The direction in which clock hands travel.

closed broken line. A figure formed when the starting point of the broken line intersects its endpoint. The *line segments* may intersect each other on the line segment. See *closed plane figure.*

closed curve. A *curve* that starts at a point and comes back to that point.

closed interval. A set of numbers consisting of two given numbers and all the numbers between them.

closed plane figure. A figure that starts at a *point* and comes back to the same point.

A simple closed figure separates the *plane* into the *set* of *points* on the figure, those outside the figure, and those inside the figure.

SIMPLE CLOSED FIGURES

NOT A SIMPLE CLOSED FIGURE

closed region. The *union* of a *simple closed curve* and its *interior*.

CLOSED REGION

closed sentence. A *sentence* in mathematics that does not contain a *variable*.

closed set. If the answer to an operation is an *element* in the given *set*, the set is closed. Set A is closed under the operations of addition and multiplication. Any two elements in the set can be added or multiplied and the sum or product is a member of set A.

Set A is the infinite set of all the counting numbers.

A = {1, 2, 3, 4, 5 . . .}

See *closure, property of*.

closed-space figure. A figure made up of a *set* of *points* in *space* that separates space into the set of points inside the figure, the set of points outside the figure, and the set of points on the figure.

CLOSED SPACE FIGURES

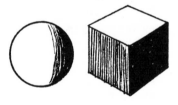

closure, property of. If a *binary operation* on any two *elements* in a given *set* produces a result that is also an element in the set, the set is said to be closed under that operation. The set of whole numbers is closed for addition and multiplication. If you take any two whole numbers, their product is another whole number. The set of whole numbers is not closed under subtraction or division. For example, $8 - 9$ is not a whole number; neither is $5 \div 3$.

cm. Abbreviation for *centimeter.*

coaxial (co-AX-ee-al). Having a common *axis.*

codes (and ciphers). Methods of writing secret messages so that they can be read only by people who know the key. The two main systems for making up codes are substitution and transposition. In substitution, the actual letters of the message are replaced by other letters, numbers, or symbols:

$$
\begin{array}{cccc}
\text{H} & \text{E} & \text{L} & \text{P} \\
8 & 5 & 12 & 16
\end{array}
$$

In transposition, the positions of the letters are changed according to some pattern. All codes can be "broken" mathematically. Computers are used for code-breaking because they can work their way through all the mathematical possibilities much more quickly than people can.

coefficient. In the *term* 5x, 5 is the coefficient of x. Generally, the coefficient is the *product* of all the *factors* of a term except one. For example, in $5x^2y$, the coefficient of y is $5x^2$.

coin-tossing. A simple way to demonstrate how *probability* works.

collateral. Property pledged for a *loan.*

collection. A *group* or *set,* such as a collection of dolls or a collection of whole numbers.

collinear (koh-LIN-ee-er) **points.** A *set* of *points* that are contained in the same line.

column. A vertical arrangement, such as a column of numbers to be added. In a *matrix,* columns are vertical and rows are horizontal.

$$
\begin{array}{c}
2 \\
3 \\
6 \\
7
\end{array}
$$

combination. Statement of addition or multiplication facts. Two whole numbers each less than 10 equal a sum or a product, depending on the operation.

$$3 + 3 = 6. 3 \times 3 = 9.$$

combinations in statistics. A set of objects selected without reference to the order in which they are arranged. If you select three out of a set of four books (titled A, B, C, and D) without regard to their order, there are four possible combinations: ABC, ABD, ACD, BCD. See *permutations*.

combining. See *union, intersection, addition*.

commensurable. Having a common *divisor* or a common measure.

commission. A fee, usually a *percentage*, given to an agent for selling a product.

common denominator. A *common multiple*, usually the *least common multiple* of the denominators of a number of *fractions*. A common denominator of

$$\frac{2}{3}, \frac{3}{4}, \frac{1}{2}$$

is their common multiple. 12.

It is also the *least common denominator* in this case.

common difference. The difference between any *term* and the preceding term of an *arithmetic progression*. For example, in the arithmetic progression 7, 11, 15, 19, the common difference is 4.

common divisor. A quantity that is a *factor* of two or more numbers, quantities or expressions.

$$3\overline{\smash{\big)}12}^{4} \qquad 3\overline{\smash{\big)}15}^{5}$$

3 IS A COMMON DIVISOR
OF 12 AND 15

common factor. A *common divisor*.

common fraction. (Also called rational number.) A *fraction* in which the *numerator* and *denominator* are both *integers*. The denominator cannot be zero.

COMMON
FRACTION $\dfrac{7}{8}$

common logarithm. *Logarithms* having 10 as a *base*. See *Briggs, Henry*.

common multiple. A *multiple* of each of two or more quantities. See *least common multiple.*

common ratio. See *geometric progression.*

commutative group (or Abelian group). A *set* of elements with the following *properties:*

    1. The system has *closure.*

    2. The *operation* is *associative.*

    3. The operation is *commutative.*

    4. It has an *identity element.*

    5. For every element there is an *inverse element.*

commutative property of addition. A law of mathematics that says the order in which you add numbers does not affect the sum. In general, for all numbers a and b, $a+b=b+a$. $4+3$ always equals $3+4$.

commutative property of multiplication. A law of mathematics that says the order in which you multiply numbers does not affect the product: $4 \times 3 = 12$, $3 \times 4 = 12$. In other words, 4×3 $= 3 \times 4$. In general, for all numbers a and b, $ab = ba$.

comparing. We may compare 8 and 2 by subtraction: 8 is 6 more than 2. We may compare them by division: 8 is 4 times as much as 2. Comparing in arithmetic usually involves the operations of subtraction and division.

comparison property. For any two numbers, 8 and 6, either $8 = 6$, $8 > 6$ (8 is greater than 6), or $8 < 6$ (8 is less than 6). In general, for any real numbers a and b, exactly one of the following statements is true: $a = b$, $a > b$, $a < b$. This is known as the ordering principle.

compass. (Also called compasses.) In geometric construction, an instrument used to draw a circle and to mark off equal lengths.

complementary angles. Two angles the sum of whose measures is a right angle.

$\angle 1$, COMPLEMENT OF $\angle 2$
$\angle 2$, COMPLEMENT OF $\angle 1$

complementary set. When a given *set* contains a *subset,* all *members* of the set not in the subset belong to the complementary set. If set A = {1, 2, 3, 4, 5}, and a subset B = {2, 3, 5}, then the complementary set to B is {1, 4}.

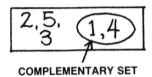

COMPLEMENTARY SET

complementation. An operation on a *set* and a *subset.* The symbol for complementation may be written A', $\sim A$, $\overline{A}$.

complete factorization of a number. The given number expressed as the *product* of *prime numbers.*

$$12 = 3 \times 2 \times 2$$

completeness. A *property* of a mathematical system in which any proposition can either be proved or disproved.

completeness property of the set of real numbers. For every point on a *number line*

there is a *real number,* and for every real number there is a point on the number line.

completing the square. A process that makes it possible to *factor* some *polynomials.* It can be used to solve any *quadratic equation.*

complex fraction. A *fraction* whose *numerator* and/or *denominator* contains fractions.

$$\frac{\frac{2}{3}}{4} \qquad \frac{\frac{x}{9}}{y} \qquad \frac{\frac{y}{2}}{\frac{3}{4}}$$

complex number. The sum of a *real number* and an *imaginary number,* such as $3 + 2i$. Complex numbers have the form $a + bi$, where a and b are real numbers and i is imaginary. The idea of complex numbers was first introduced by Italian mathematicians in the sixteenth century.

component. A part; in an *ordered pair,* the object that occurs first is the first component and the object that occurs

$$(2,3)$$

↖ FIRST COMPONENT

↑

SECOND
COMPONENT

second is the second component.

composite number. A whole number such as 8, 36, or 100 that is not a *prime number*.

compound condition. Two *simple conditions* combined by a *connective*.

$$x > 3 \land x < 5$$

X IS GREATER   AND   X IS LESS
THAN 3   THAN 5

$$OR: 3 < 4 \land 4 < 5$$

compound event. In *probability*, two or more independent, but not all, of the possible events in an occurrence.

compound interest. *Interest* paid not only on the *principal* of a sum but also on the interest that has been added to the principle.

compound number. A quantity expressed in more than one unit or denomination, as 2 feet 6 inches.

compound sentence. A sentence constructed from two or more *simple sentences*. For example, $3 + 4 = 7$ or $9 - 6 = 2$. This is a true sentence, because one part of it is true. But if "or" is changed to "and," $3 + 4 = 7$ and $9 - 6 = 2$, then it is a false sentence.

Comptometer (kom-TOM-e-tur). A trade name for the first successful calculating machine built, in 1887, to handle more than one column of digits at a time.

computation. The act or method of carrying out a mathematical process.

computer. An electronic device capable of manipulating a great deal of information (data) in a very short time; manipulating the data put into it with a set of rules called a *program*, and returning results in a fraction of a second. The *input* information could be typewriter keystrokes, voice commands, digitalized optical images, any kind of numbers or measurements, or signals from other computers. *Output* information can be displayed in any of those forms and can be stored for future use. Computers can also generate drawings or plans, and give directions to other computers or to machines. A computer has *chips* with the ability to do binary calculations. It has a memory that can continually get stored information and use it. It has a process controller that tells it where to find things and where to put them. Its compiler processes the data and reformats it in a way that people or machines can understand. Most computers are digital. Analog computers are used only for very special purposes. Their output is usually translated to be used by a digital computer.

Supercomputers convert numbers into two- or three-dimensional color pictures or movies on the computer screen. By using images instead of numbers, scientists can visualize data, move images around and recognize patterns that are hard to detect in columns of figures.

Charles Babbage had the first idea for making an automatic digital computer about 1835. *Lord Kelvin* had the first idea for an analog computer in 1876. *Vannevar Bush* built the first large analog computer in 1931. Howard Aiken built the first digital computer in 1944. J. Prosper Eckert and John W. Mauchly built the first all-electronic computer in 1946. *John von Neumann* contributed much to the design of today's computers. He developed the idea of stored programs.

concentric circles. Two or more circles in one *plane,* having the same *point* as their center.

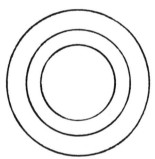

CONCENTRIC CIRCLES

concept. A mental impression or an idea and all its associations.

conclusion. The final statement in a *proof,* which follows from previous statements.

concrete number. Belonging to actual objects; opposed to *abstract number.* A number is concrete if it refers to specific objects, such as 2 books.

concurrent lines. Two or more lines with a *point* in common.

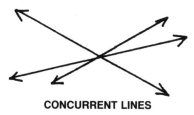

CONCURRENT LINES

condition. See *simple condition, compound condition.*

conditional equation. An *equation* with one or more *variables.* In an equation such as $3x - 1 = 5$, a true statement is formed only if 2 is the replacement for x. 2 is the solution for the equation. The fact that $x = 2$ is the condition that makes the equation true.

Equations that are true for some but not all values of the variable or variables are called conditional equations. $x + y = 7$ is true for a number of pairs of values, but not true for other pairs of values. See *identical equation.*

conditional open sentence (or implication). A sentence formed by joining two sentences in the form "if . . . then." The first sentence is the *hypothesis* (antecedent), and the second sentence is the *conclusion* (consequent). In the implication, "If $3 + 3 = 6$, then $4 + 3 = 7$," $3 + 3 = 6$ is the hypothesis and $4 + 3 = 7$ is the conclusion. A conditional is usually written in the form: "if p then q," or $p \rightarrow q$. $p \rightarrow q$ is true except where p is true and q is false.

cone. A *solid* bounded by a conical *surface* and a *plane* cutting all elements. If the base is a circle, we call it a circular cone. If the base is

CONE

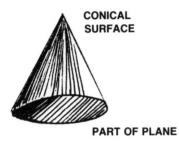

**CONICAL
SURFACE**

PART OF PLANE

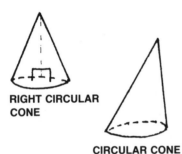

**RIGHT CIRCULAR
CONE**

CIRCULAR CONE

perpendicular to its *axis*, it is
a right circular cone. See *table of formulas, p. 241.*

confidence level or confidence coefficient. A term
used in testing *hypotheses*. If
a 95% confidence level is
used, the *probability* of an
event occurring by chance is
5 out of 100.

configuration. The way the
elements in anything are arranged.

congruent figures. Two or
more *plane figures* that have

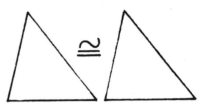

the same size and shape. See
also *corresponding angles,
sides, vertices.*

congruent numbers. Two
numbers that have the same
remainder when they are each
divided by a third number
(called a *modulus*). For example, 7 and 9 are congruent,
modulus 2. This is written
$7 \equiv 9 \pmod{2}$.

conic sections (KON-ik).
From ancient times. Curves
formed by the intersection of
a *plane* and a right circular

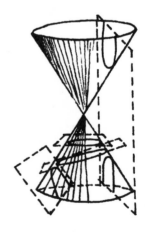

cone. Depending on where the plane cuts through, the conic section may be a *circle,* an *ellipse,* a *parabola,* or a *hyperbola.* It may even be a straight line, a pair of straight lines, or a point.

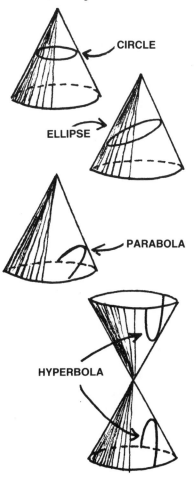

conjunction of equations. A *compound sentence,* such as $x + y = 7$ and $x - y = 3$. This is true only when $x = 5$ and $y = 2$. See *connective.*

connective. A word or symbol used to combine two or more sentences into one sentence. See *and; or; conditional open sentence.*

consequent. See *hypothesis, conditional open sentence, conclusion.*

consistent. A set of *assumptions* or *hypotheses* that do not contradict each other.

consistent equations. *Equations* having one solution in common.

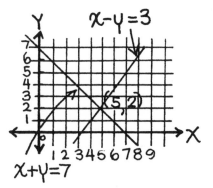

constant. An absolute constant is a number that always has the same value, like the number 10. In $3x^2 + 5$, 5 is the constant. An arbitrary constant has a particular value in a particular problem. Arbitrary constants are usually represented by letters from the beginning of the alphabet—a, b, c, etc. See *variable*.

constant factor. See *geometric progression*.

construction. The drawing of a figure in geometry, usually with *straightedge* and *compass*, to fulfill the conditions that describe it.

contiguous (kon-TIG-you-us). In geometry, next to and touching.

CONTIGUOUS ANGLES

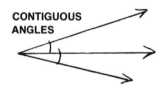

continued fraction. A number plus a fractional number whose *denominator* is a num-

$$\frac{26}{11} = 2 + \frac{1}{2 + \frac{1}{1 + \frac{1}{3}}}$$

ber plus a fractional number, and so on. See *fraction*.

continuity. A fundamental concept in *algebra, geometry,* and *topology* saying there are no "holes" in a line; the line extends in a continuous fashion with no breaks. See *density*.

continuous. Flowing, without a break. See *discrete*.

continuous curve. A *curve* that is not broken into two or more parts.

continuous data. *Data* obtained from a moving sheet of paper on which a line is drawn to show the changes taking place every moment.

continuous numbers. A *set* of *real numbers* that can be put into a *one-to-one correspondence* with every *point* on a *number line*. The *rational numbers* are not continuous.

continuum (kon-TIN-you-um). An *infinite set* of numbers or objects between any two other numbers or objects. The set of all *real numbers* is called the continuum of real numbers. Any *closed interval*

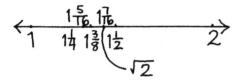

of real numbers is a continuum. An infinite set of numbers can be inserted between any two numbers, 1 and 2, for example, and there are no gaps in the line.

contour. The outline of any figure or body.

contradiction or contradictory statement. Two statements. If one can be proved false, the other must be true.

contrapositive. A statement formed by reversing the order and negating the parts of an *"if . . . then"* statement. For example, if two angles of a triangle are not equal, the sides opposite these angles are not equal. If two sides of a triangle are not equal, the angles opposite these sides are not equal.

converging lines. *Lines* that meet at a *point.*

converse of a statement. If a statement says, "If p then q," the converse would be,

"If q then p." For example, "If the triangle is *isosceles,* it has two equal angles." The converse is, "If the triangle has two equal angles, it is an isosceles triangle."

conversion table. A table comparing units in two different systems. For the conversion table of metric units into English units, see *p. 249.*

coordinates (koh-ORD-i-nits). If a number is associated with a *point* on a *line,* the number is called the coordinate of the point. If an *ordered pair* of

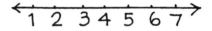

numbers is associated with a point on a plane, the numbers are called coordinates of the point. For point P, 3 is the x-coordinate and 2 is the y-coordinate. See *abscissa, or-*

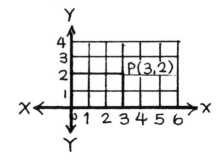

dinate, Cartesian coordinates. Latitude and *longitude* use coordinates to locate points on the sphere of the earth.

Copernicus (koh-PURR-nik-us) **Nicholas,** 1473–1543. A Polish astronomer, mathematician, doctor, and lawyer whose description of our solar system is the basis of modern astronomy. He believed that the sun was the center of the universe, and the earth and other planets revolved around it.

coplanar (ko-PLAIN-ur) **points.** *Points* that lie on the same *plane*. A *square* is a *set* of coplanar points.

cord. A measure of a volume of wood, 128 cubic feet, usually arranged $4' \times 8' \times 4'$. See *table, p. 245.*

corollary (CORE-a-ler-ee). A *theorem* that follows directly from the *proof* of another theorem.

correction. A quantity or number that must be applied to ensure accuracy in the solution of a problem, such as mapping a course with a marine compass.

correspondence. A one-to-one relationship between sets. Every element in one set can be matched with one and only one element in another set, and every element in the second set can be matched with one and only one element of the first set. There are also

$$\text{SET A} = \{A, B\ C\ D\}$$
$$\text{SET B} = \{1, 2, 3, 4\}$$

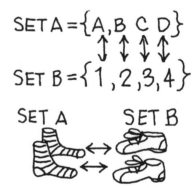

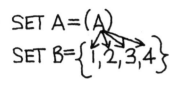

many correspondences where one element in a set relates to a number of elements in another set.

corresponding angles. If two lines are cut by a transversal the corresponding pairs of angles are $\angle 1$ and $\angle 5$; $\angle 3$ and $\angle 7$; $\angle 2$ and $\angle 6$; $\angle 4$ and $\angle 8$.

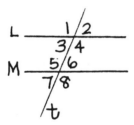

In the *congruent* triangles below, $\angle B$ and $\angle E$, $\angle A$ and $\angle D$, $\angle C$ and $\angle F$ are congruent to each other. They are pairs of corresponding angles in the congruent triangles.

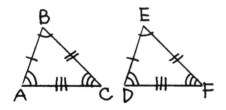

corresponding sides. In two similar or *congruent* triangles, such as the triangles below, $\overline{AB}$ and $\overline{DE}$ are corresponding sides. So are $\overline{BC}$ and $\overline{EF}$, and $\overline{AC}$ and $\overline{DF}$.

corresponding vertices. In the similar or *congruent* triangles ABC and DEF, the *vertices* A and D, B and E, and C and F are corresponding vertices.

cosecant (koh-SEE-kant). In a right-angle triangle, the *ratio* of the length of the *hypotenuse* to the side opposite an *acute angle*. The cosecant of angle A is usually abbreviated cosec A and is equal to the *reciprocal* of its *sine*.

cosine. In a right-angle triangle, the *ratio* of the length of the side adjacent to an acute angle to the length of the *hypotenuse*. The cosine of angle A is usually abbreviated cos A.

cost. The price charged for something. The amount of money paid for an object or service.

cost formula. See *table of formulas, p. 243.*

cotangent.

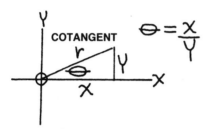

coulomb (koo-LOM). A unit of electric charge that measures the amount of electricity flowing over the period of a second when the current is I *ampere*. The word comes from the name of the French physicist, Charles Coulomb.

counterclockwise. In the opposite direction to the way clock hands travel.

counting. *Assigning* to every member of a *set* a number in an ordered *sequence*. The last number assigned is the *cardinal number* of the set.

counting numbers. The set of numbers 1, 2, 3, 4, 5 · · ·

counting system. Any system for putting numerals or objects in order, to work with them one at a time.

credit. Power to buy or borrow on trust; the balance in an account.

cross. A symbol for an *operation* on *sets*. A x B is read "A cross B," or "the *Cartesian product* of A and B."

cryptogram (KRIPT-oh-gram). Same as *code*.

cube. A *solid*. A physical model of a cube is the outside of a child's block. A cube has twelve equal edges, each edge perpendicular to its adjoining edges. The six faces of a cube are parts of *planes* bounded by squares.

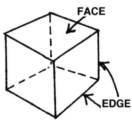

cube. To raise a quantity to the third *power*. 5^3 may be read 5 cubed, or 5 cube, or 5 to the third power. 5^3 means $5 \times 5 \times 5$, or 125.

cube problem. The problem of constructing a second cube having twice the volume of a given cube. In the nineteenth century a solution to the problem with *straightedge* and *compass* was proved impossible.

cube root. The *inverse* process of raising to a *cube*. If $(2)^3 = 8$, then $\sqrt[3]{8} = 2$. In general, for every number a, $\sqrt[3]{a}$ is the number whose cube is a.

$\sqrt[3]{a}$ is positive if a is positive.

$\sqrt[3]{a}$ is negative if a is negative.

$\sqrt[3]{a}$ is zero if a is zero.

cubic centimeter. In the metric system, $\frac{1}{1000}$ of a *liter*.

cubic equations. *Equations* in which the highest sum of *exponents* of the *variables* is 3.

cubic foot. 1,728 cubic inches, or 28.3 *liters*.

cubic measure. A measure of *volume*. See *table, p. 245.*

cubic yard. 27 cubic feet.

Cuisenaire (KWEEZ-in-air) **rods.** A set of colored rods of different but related lengths to help children learn number concepts and ways to operate on numbers. For example, white is 1 and vermillion, which is twice as long, is 2. Together they are the same length as light green, which is 3.

$$1 + 2 = 3.$$

cup. The symbol for *union* of *sets*. A ∪ B is read, "A cup B," or "the union of A and B." See *join.*

curvature. The rate at which the direction of the curve changes per unit along the curve.

curve. An uninterrupted *set* of *points*. There are open curves and closed curves.

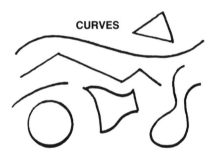

CURVES

curve of distribution. See *bell-shaped curve.*

curve, simple. A curve that does not cross itself. A simple curve may look complicated. It may be open or closed.

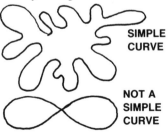

SIMPLE CURVE

NOT A SIMPLE CURVE

cybernetics (SY-bur-NET-iks). The processes of thinking, problem solving, communications, etc., in people and machines.

cycle. An interval of time in which some regular event takes place.

cycloid (SY-kloyd). A curve traced by a *point,* as on the rim of a wheel as the wheel rolls along a straight *line* in one *plane.*

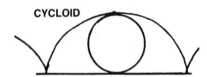

CYCLOID

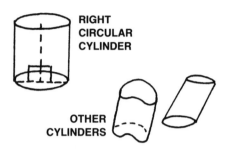

RIGHT CIRCULAR CYLINDER

OTHER CYLINDERS

cylinder. A solid. A can is a physical model of a right circular cylinder. It consists of a cylindrical *surface* perpendicular to two parallel *circular closed regions.* The right circular cylinder is the one we usually see in our physical world. However, there are other kinds of cylinders, too.

D

D. The capital letter D is the Roman numeral for 500.

d. A symbol for *distance* and for *diameter*. It is used in the formula d = rt.

D'Alembert (dahl-ahm-BEAR), **Jean,** 1717–1783. French mathematician, astronomer, and philosopher. He was particularly interested in integral calculus and in Newton's laws of motion. He formulated the D'Alembert test for convergence of an infinite series and the D'Alembert principle, which states that the forces in an object that resist acceleration must be equal and opposite to the forces that produce the acceleration.

data. Related facts or information, usually numerical, often arranged in charts or graphs to show the relationship between them.

data base. A large collection of information about any one subject.

data base management. The capability to organize all kinds of data.

date line, international. An imaginary line on the surface

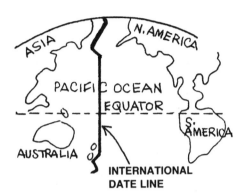

INTERNATIONAL DATE LINE

of the earth, running roughly along the 180th meridian. By international agreement, at midnight along the international date line, a day ends on the eastern side and a new day begins on the western side.

day. The twenty-four-hour period of time it takes the earth to rotate once on its axis.

debenture (deh-BEN-chur). A statement of debt. The value of a debenture bond depends on the credit of the issuer.

debit. In bookkeeping, the cost of an item, which is marked on an account or ledger sheet as something owed.

deca. (DEKKA). Prefix meaning 10.

decade. A period of ten years.

decagon (DEK-a-gon). A *polygon* having ten sides.

decagram. 10 *grams* in the *metric system*. See *table, p. 248.*

decahedron. A *polyhedron* with ten faces or sides.

DECAHEDRON

decaliter. 10 *liters* in the *metric system*.

decameter. 10 *meters* in the *metric system*.

deci. Prefix meaning one-tenth.

decibel. A unit for measuring the loudness of sound; 1/10 of a *bel*. A painfully loud sound is about 120 decibels; a barely audible sound is 0 decibel.

decigram. 1/10 of a *gram* in the *metric system*.

deciliter. 1/10 of a *liter* in the *metric system*.

decillion (dih-SILL-yun). In the United States and France, the *cardinal number* 1 followed by 33 zeros; in England and Germany, 1 followed by 60 zeros.

decimal equivalent of a fraction. A decimal fraction equal to a *common fraction*. ¾ = .75.

decimal fraction. A *fractional number* may be expressed in decimal form. Seven-tenths may be 7/10 or .7. In .7 the denominator is not written but understood. The dot in .7 is called a *decimal point*.

.4 is four-tenths
.04 is four-hundredths

decimal, nonterminating. *Decimal fractions* are often used to approximate the value of *common fractions*.

⅓ = .3333 . . .

There are two kinds of nonterminating decimals: In .3333 . . . the digit 3 repeats. It is called a repeating, nonterminating decimal. A decimal approximation for π is

3.14159 . . . This is a nonterminating decimal that does not repeat.

decimal point. A dot or point that separates a *decimal fraction* from the whole numbers. When reading decimal fractions, the decimal point is read as "and." The decimal point was first used in the early seventeenth century. It is written differently in different countries:

In the United States, 2.37
In England, 2·37
In France and Germany, 2,37

decimal, terminating. In ¼ = .25 we sometimes call .25 a *terminating* decimal. However, .25 can be considered .25000 . . . with the 0 repeating. See *decimal, nonterminating.*

decimals, changing to fractional numerals. A decimal numeral such as .6 may be written as a fractional numeral by using the denominator that indicates the place value correctly.

$$.6 = ^6/_{10}$$

Any *nonterminating, repeating decimal* can be expressed in fractional form. See *fraction.*

decimals, changing to percent. Any decimal can be expressed as a percent. For example,

$$.6 = 60\%$$
$$.06 = 6\%$$
$$.625 = 62\frac{1}{2}\% \text{ or } 62.5\%$$

decimal system. Any numeration system with a *base* of ten.

decimeter. One-tenth of a *meter* in the *metric system,* or ten *centimeters.* See *table, p. 248.*

Dedekind (DED-ih-kint), **Richard,** 1831–1916. German mathematician, a member of the "German school," which included *Cantor.* He did much work on irrational numbers and infinite classes. He invented the *infinite* class of algebraic numbers called ideals and the Dedekind cut in the theory of *irrational numbers.*

deduce. To reach a conclusion based on certain known *data.*

deduct. To take away, or *subtract.*

deduction. A result or conclusion based on a set of statements, each of which is justified by a *postulate,* is given to be true, or is based on a *theorem* previously proved.

deductive reasoning. The method of reasoning whereby a general statement is applied to a particular case. For example:

1. All students must take two years of mathematics in order to receive a diploma. (A general statement.)

2. Henry is a student who wishes to receive a diploma. (A specific statement.)

3. He must take two years of mathematics. (Conclusion.) See *syllogism.*

deductive system. A set of undefined *terms, definitions, assumptions* or *postulates* is used to deduce *theorems* through the application of the laws of logic.

Dee, John, (1527–1608). Mathematician, astronomer, and astrologer to Queen Elizabeth I of England.

defective number. Same as *deficient number.*

deficient number. A *whole number* in which the sum of its *factors* (except itself) is less than the number itself. 16 is a deficient number; its factors, 1, 2, 4 and 8, add up to 15.

deficit. The amount by which a sum (usually money) is short of a required amount.

definition, mathematical. An agreement about the meaning of words and symbols used in mathematics.

degree. In geometry, a degree is a unit of angular measure. A straight angle measures 180°; a right angle 90°.

In temperature measurement, a degree is a unit of temperature. Normal human body temperature is 98.6° *Fahrenheit;* the freezing point of water is 32°F, 0° *Celsius.*

Of a *monomial.* The degree of a monomial is the sum of the *exponents* of the *variables.* If there is no variable, the degree is 0.

The degree of $3x$ is 1.
The degree of $5x^2$ is 2.
The degree of $2x^2y^3$ is 5.
The degree of 4 is 0.

Of a *polynomial*. The degree of the monomial term of highest degree. The degree of $9x^3 + 4x^2 - 7x + 2$ is 3.

degree of an equation. The *degree* of $2a + b = 5$ is an *equation* of the first degree. It is called a linear equation, because its graph is a line. $3x^2 + 5 = 17$ is an equation of the second degree, called a *quadratic equation*. See *analytic geometry*.

degree of an expression. See *degree*.

deka (or deca). Prefix meaning ten.

delta. The fourth letter of the Greek alphabet and the Greek numeral for 4. It was written δ or Δ and called delta. When written Δy, we read it as the difference of the y-coordinates.

de Méré, Antoine Lombard, Chevalier, 1610–1684. A French gambler and friend of *Fermat* and *Pascal*. He asked them to solve this problem mathematically: If a certain number of points were needed to win an unfinished dice game, with one player ahead, how could the stakes be divided fairly?

Solving this problem started Pascal on his famous *probability* research, the result of which was the *Pascal triangle* of probability.

Democritus (de-MOK-rih-tus), 460–370 B.C. Greek scientist and mathematician, known chiefly as the originator of the atomic theory of the structure of the universe. He is supposed to be the first mathematician to state the formula for finding the volume of a cone or a pyramid. His theories foreshadowed the work of *Archimedes* and provided the beginning of infinitesimal calculus.

DeMoivre, Abraham, 1667–1754. French mathematician, friend of *Newton,* and one of the group who investigated the dispute between Newton and *Leibniz.* He worked in trigonometry but is best known for his "Doctrine of Chances," a study of *probability.* He also helped form the idea of a normal curve of distribution. DeMoivre's theorem is a rule for raising a complex number to a power.

DeMorgan, Augustus, 1806–1871. English mathematician and logician, a noted teacher, and founder of the London Mathematical Society. He wrote on probability, trigonometry, and paradoxes. DeMorgan's rule is used in *set* theory.

denominate number. A number that refers to a special unit of measurement: 7 inches, 25 dollars, 19 pounds. A compound denominate number refers to two sets of measurements, such as 6 feet 5 inches.

denominator. In $2/5$, the 5 is the denominator.

density of matter. A unit volume of mass that shows the number of pounds per cubic feet, or grams per cubic centimeter.

density property. When we say the *set* of *rational numbers* is dense, we mean that it is always possible to find other rational numbers between any two rational numbers.

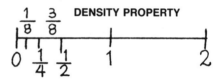

DENSITY PROPERTY

Between 0 and 1 there is $1/2$.
Between 0 and $1/2$ there is $1/4$.
Between 0 and $1/4$ there is $1/8$.

denumerable (de-NOOM-er-a-bull). A *set* that can be counted or put into *one-to-one correspondence* with the *natural numbers.*

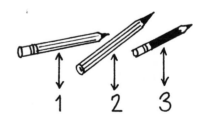

dependent equations. Two *equations* such as $x + y = 3$ and $4x + 4y = 12$ have many common solutions. Any pair of numbers that *satisfies* one equation satisfies the other. Their graphs are the same line. Such a system of equations is called a dependent system.

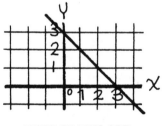

DEPENDENT EQUATIONS

IF $x + y = 3$
AND $4x + 4y = 12$
x COULD BE y

0	3
1	2
2	1

AND MORE

**THEIR GRAPHS ARE
THE SAME LINE**

dependent variable. In the *function* $y = 3x$, the value of y, when $x = 2$, is 6. y is sometimes called the dependent variable, with x as the independent variable. Of course, if $y = 6$, then x is 2. See *function*.

depreciation. Loss in value of goods or property, or a decrease in the value of money.

depressed equation. An *equation*, not in common use, whose *degree* is less than the original equation. It is the result of reducing the number of *roots* of an equation. For example, given $x^2 + 2x - 3 = 0$, if both members are divided by $x - 1$, the result is the depressed equation $x + 3 = 0$.

Desargues (duh-SARG), **Gérard,** 1593–1662. French engineer and architect whose theories on conics had a great effect on the work of *Descartes* and *Pascal*. He was one of a new group of mathematicians who realized that Greek geometry could not be pursued much further, and who looked for new ways of extending the scope of geometry. He formulated important ideas in projective geometry.

Descartes (day-KART), **René,** 1596–1650. French mathematician, philosopher, and scientist, often called, "the father of modern mathematics." Descartes's main contribution to mathematics was his invention of *Cartesian* or *analytic geometry,* which united algebra and geometry. This enabled mathematicians to map any equation as a set of points on a *graph.*

Descartes learned that the graph of a first-degree equation makes a straight line; the graph of a second-degree equation makes a circle and other conic sections, and the higher the degree of the equation, the more complex the curve on the graph. He also demonstrated that if an equation could be graphed as a line, a line could be written as an equation.

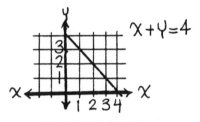

GRAPH OF A FIRST-DEGREE EQUATION

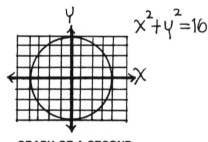

GRAPH OF A SECOND-DEGREE EQUATION

Descartes tried to determine how many roots of an equation are positive and how many are negative. A rule for determining the upper limit to the number of positive and negative roots, based upon variations in signs, is called Descartes's rule of signs, although the discovery was actually made by *Harriot*.

descending order. In $3x^4 + 4x^3 - 3x^2 + 2x + 7$, the terms of the *polynomial* are written in descending order. The term with the highest power of the *variable* is first (at the left) and the term with the next highest is second, and so on.

description of a set. A set may be described by listing its members: $A = \{1, 2, 3, 4, 5\}$. It may be described by a condition, such as "the set of natural numbers less than 6." This is also called the set roster.

determinant. A square array of elements that shows the sum of the *products*.

$$\begin{vmatrix} 3 & 2 \\ 5 & 6 \end{vmatrix} = 18 - 10 = 8$$

development (or net). The *plane geometric* figure obtained by opening up and flattening a *solid* figure without

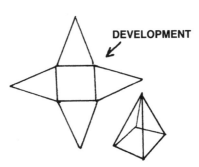

DEVELOPMENT

changing the area of its surfaces.

deviation from the mean. In statistics, a measure of the variation from the trend. If the mean (average) of a set of numbers is 80 and one *member* of the set is 75, we say that its deviation from the mean is 5.

deviation, standard. A statistic that characterizes a *distribution* of *scores*. See *central tendency*.

diagonal. A *line segment* connecting two nonadjacent *vertices* of a *polygon*.

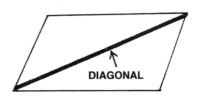

DIAGONAL

diagram 80 **dilation**

diagram. A drawing showing data, geometric figures, etc.

diameter. A *line segment* that contains the center of a circle and whose *endpoints* are on the circle. A *chord* that contains the center of the *circle.* See *table of formulas, p. 240.*

difference. The amount by which one quantity or number is greater or less than another. The mathematical *operation* for finding differences is *subtraction* and the symbol is a *minus* sign $-$. See also *absolute difference.*

difference engine. The first machine designed by *Charles Babbage,* in 1822. It was actually an adding machine designed to compute and print tables automatically, and was accurate to six decimal places. The machine was never completed, though the British government contributed about 17,000 pounds (an enormous sum in those days) toward it, because engineering techniques of the time were not sufficiently advanced.

differential calculus. A branch of mathematics that may be applied to such problems as finding the speed of a given object at a given time, or the steepness of a curve at any point. It is also known as the calculus of change, or fluxions. See *Newton; Leibniz.*

digit. The ten digits in our numeration system are 0, 1, 2, 3, 4, 5, 6, 7, 8, and 9. The word comes from the Latin *digitus,* meaning "finger" or "toe."

digital computer. See *computer.*

dihedral (die-HEED-rul) **angle.** The *angle* made by two intersecting planes. The two planes are called the faces and the line of intersection is called the edge.

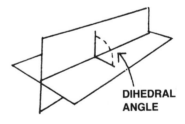

DIHEDRAL ANGLE

dilation. The transformation property that permits a geometric figure to contract or

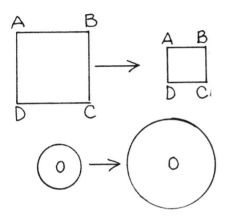

**PROPERTIES OF SQUARE ABCD
AND CIRCLE O ARE THE SAME, EVEN
THOUGH THEIR SIZES CHANGE**

expand; an *invariant* property of *Euclidean geometry.*

dime. A U.S. coin equal to 10 cents, $\frac{1}{10}$ of a dollar.

dimension. A measure. *Points* are considered to have no di-

NO DIMENSION

←———————→ ONE DIMENSION

TWO DIMENSIONS

THREE DIMENSIONS

mension; *line segments* have length, or one dimension; *plane figures* have area, or two dimensions; *solids* have volume, or three dimensions. *Albert Einstein* said that time is a fourth dimension. Some scientists think that there might be ten or more dimensions in the universe. See *super-string theory.*

Diophantus (dy-oh-FAN-tus), ?–A.D. 320? A member, along with *Hero* and *Pappus,* of the Second Alexandrian School. He wrote thirteen books forming the *Arithmetica,* of which six survive. They are the earliest known works on algebra. His chief contribution was the introduction of a new notation using contractions of words or symbols to stand for unknown quantities and operations. Until that time the Greeks had used all the letters of the alphabet for particular numbers and had no way to represent unknown quantities.

directed line segment. A *line segment* in which one *endpoint* is designated the initial point and the other endpoint is the terminal point. The seg-

INITIAL POINT

TERMINAL POINT

DIRECTED LINE SEGMENT AB

ment is directed from the first endpoint to the second.

directed numbers. Also called *signed numbers.* Geometrically, numbers are associated with points on a line. Zero is associated with a point, then numbers are associated with the points to the left and right of it. Numbers to the right of the zero point are called *positive numbers;*

$$-3 \ -2 \ -1 \ \ 0 \ +1 \ +2 \ +3$$

those to the left are called *negative numbers.* Sometimes, instead of *plus* or *minus* signs, the signed numerals have arrows pointing to the right for positive and to the left for negative.

$$\leftarrow \quad \rightarrow$$
$$3 \quad 5$$

direct proportion. See *direct variation.*

direct variation. In a set of ordered number pairs $\{(10, 2)$

$(15, 3) (20, 4)\}$, for any value except zero, the quotient of any pair is constant:

$$\frac{10}{2} = 5, \frac{15}{3} = 5, \frac{20}{4} = 5$$

When the *ratio* is the same for any pair in a set of pairs, the set of pairs is a direct variation.

POSSIBLE PAIRS OF VALUES FOR Y = 5x

x	y
1	5
2	10
3	15
4	20
5	25

discount. An amount deducted from a bill. The rate of discount is usually given as a percent.

discrete. Separate or distinct. The points on a line associated with the *natural numbers* are discrete. The opposite of discrete is *continuous.*

disjoint sets. The *set* of boys in a class and the set of girls in a class are said to be disjoint because there is no member which belongs to both sets.

disjunction. A *compound sentence* formed by joining two *simple statements* with "or" is called a disjunction. "It is raining or the game is being played," is an example of a disjunction. In mathematical statements, the symbol for the disjunction "or" is "$\vee$": $5 < x \vee 5 = x$. For a disjunction to be true, one or both simple statements must be true. See *connective*.

distance. See *table of formulas, p. 243*.

distance on a number line. The *absolute value* of the difference between the *coordinates* of any two *points*.

$$A \qquad B$$
$$\overleftrightarrow{4\ 5\ 6\ 7\ 8\ 9\ 10}$$
$$AB = |4 - 9| = 5$$
$$\text{OR}$$
$$AB = |9 - 4| = 5$$

distribution. In statistics, an arrangement of a set of values. The picture shows a *frequency* distribution. *Binomial*

MARKS	FREQUENCY
90-100	III
80-90	⦀⦀⦀ I
70-80	IIII
60-70	II

distribution is used in *probability*. See *binomial theorem*.

distribution curve (frequency curve). In statistics, the graph made from a frequency distribution. A normal distribution curve is usually *bell-shaped*, with the greatest number of scores clustering near the middle of the curve. If the distribution or *frequency curve* is "off center," for example, as in one showing ages at which people marry, it is called a *skewed curve*.

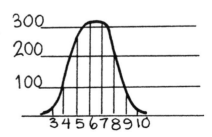

SHOE SIZES IN GIRLS' STORES

distributive property of multiplication over addition. In the *real number* system, this is a link between the operation of addition and multiplication. In $2 \times 14 = 28$, 2 and 14 are *factors* and 28 is their *product*. 14 may be renamed $10 + 4$. $2 \times (10 + 4)$ is the same as $2 \times 10 + 2 \times 4$. In general, for numbers a, b, and c, this property is written $a(b + c) = ab + ac$. For example, $2 \times (4 + 5) = 2 \times 4 + 2 \times 5$, or 18.

A *factor* can be written as the sum of two addends.

dividend. In the operation of division, the number that is to be divided by another number. A dividend is also a sum of money paid to stockholders of a company from earnings, or to insured persons from the profits of an insurance company.

divisible. When a number is divided by another number so that the remainder is zero, the first number is said to be divisible by the second.

divisibility, tests for. A number is divisible by 2 if the end digit on the right side is 0, 2, 4, 6 or 8.

A number is divisible by 3 if the sum of the value of all the digits in the numeral is divisible by 3.

A number is divisible by 4 if the value of the last two right-hand digits is divisible by 4.

A number is divisible by 5 if it ends in 5 or 0.

A number is divisible by 6 if it is even and if the sum of the value of its digits is divisible by 3.

To find if a number is divisible by 7, you need a key number, 132. For example, to test 17703, write the numbers in reverse order, multiplying them by the key, like this:

$$1\,7\,7\,0\,3$$
$$(3 \cdot 1 + 0 \cdot 3 + 7 \cdot 2) - (7 \cdot 1 + 1 \cdot 3 + 0 \cdot 2)$$
$$17 \qquad 10$$
$$7$$

If the answer is 7 or a simple multiple of 7, the number is divisible by 7.

A number is usually divisible by 8 if the sum of the value of its last three digits is divisible by 8, or if the last three digits are zeros.

A number is divisible by 9 if the sum of the value of its digits is divisible by 9.

To find if a number is divisible by 11, rewrite the digits of the number in reverse order, alternating signs. For example, to test 96811, write $1 - 1 + 8 - 6 + 9$ and do the arithmetic. If the sum is 0 or 11, the number is divisible by 11.

division. An *operation* on numbers, the *inverse* of multiplication. For example, $18 \div 2 = 9$ means $9 \times 2 = 18$. If one factor is unknown, as in $\square \times 2 = 18$, the factor may be found as $\frac{18}{2}$ or 9. In general, $a \div b = c$ means $c \times b = a$. Division by zero is meaningless. For example, $\frac{6}{0}$ is meaningless.

$$\frac{6}{0} = ? \quad \frac{10}{1} = 10 \quad \frac{0}{6} = 0$$

division property of equality. If both members of an *equation* are divided by the same number (other than zero), the resulting equation is *equivalent* to the original one. In general, if $a = b$ then

$$\frac{a}{c} = \frac{b}{c} \qquad \frac{9x}{9} = \frac{18}{9}$$

$x = 2$; $9x = 18$; $9 \cdot 2 = 18$ true.

divisor. The number by which the *dividend* is to be divided.

$$\frac{24}{6} = 4$$

divisor, common (or *common factor*). A common divisor of 18 and 27 is 3. But the *greatest common divisor* or factor of these numbers is 9.

dodecagon (doh-DEK-a-gon). A *polygon* having twelve sides.

dodecahedron (doh-dek-a-HEE-dron). A *polyhedron* having twelve faces. In ancient times it was the symbol of the universe.

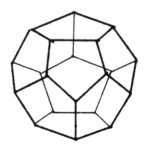

Dodgson, Charles. See *Carroll, Lewis.*

dollar. The basic monetary unit of the United States, equal to 100 *cents.*

domain of a relation. A relation is a set of *ordered pairs.* The domain is the set of first members of those ordered pairs. The *range* is the set of second members of the ordered pairs of a relation. See *function.*

$$A = \{(1,2),(3,4),(5,6),(7,8)\}$$

$$\text{DOMAIN} = \{1,3,5,7\}$$

$$\text{RANGE} = \{2,4,6,8\}$$

domain of a variable. The set of all possible replacements for a *variable.* The domain may be a *finite set* or an *infinite set.*

dot matrix. Computer printing made up of closely spaced dots.

double. Twice as much.

double-entry bookkeeping. A method of recording business transactions by making each entry twice, once to the credit of one account and once to the debit of another.

dozen (abbreviation, doz.). 12 units, as a dozen eggs.

dram. 60 grains or ⅛ oz. in *apothecaries' weight.* See *table, p. 244.*

dry measure. Part of the *avoirdupois system,* used to measure such things as fruit and grain. See *table, p. 244.*

duodecimal (doo-oh-DES-ih-mul) **numeration system.** A system with a *base* of 12. (Our *decimal system* has a base of 10). A base twelve system would need two new basic symbols. Some people believe the duodecimal system superior to a base ten system because 12 is divisible by 2, 3, 4 and 6.

0,1,2,3,4,5,6,7,8,9
0,1,2,3,4,5,6,7,8,9,T(en), E(leven)

A BASE TWELVE SYSTEM WOULD NEED TWO NEW NUMERALS

duplication of the cube. See *cube problem.*

Dürer, Albrecht, 1471–1528. A German artist and mathematician. His chief mathe-

matical work, discussing perspective and geometry, appeared in 1525. One of his most famous engravings, "Melancholia," contains an order four *magic square* that has often been copied. He also gave a construction that is a very good approximation for the *trisection* of an angle, using only *Euclidean tools*.

dyadic (dy-ADD-ik) **notation.** See *binary system*.

dyne. A small unit of force that, acting on a mass of 1 gram, gives it an acceleration of 1 centimeter per second.

E

E. The capital letter E is the abbreviation for energy. $E = mc^2$ is the formula that expresses the *Einstein* theory of relativity.

e. The lowercase e is a symbol for a *transcendental number*. The value of e is approximately 2.7182818 . . . It is used as the base of natural *logarithms*. See *Napier*.

edge. The straight *line segment* that is the intersection of two plane *faces* of a *solid*, as the edges of a *cube*.

Egyptians, mathematics of. The Egyptians were good mathematicians 5,000 years ago. We think they knew how to form right triangles by using knotted ropes.

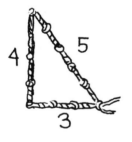

The Egyptians were practical mathematicians. They used their mathematics for measuring land, building magnificent structures that are still standing, and for studying the stars in order to calculate the timing of the seasons. Their numeration system looked like this:

I II III IIII III III IIII IIII III
II III III IIII III
III

1 2 3 4 5 6 7 8 9

∩   ⊙   ⟋   ⟨

10   100   1000   10,000

⟋⟨

100,000   1,000,000

Einstein, Albert, 1879–1955. One of the greatest scientists of all time. Born in Germany, he became a Swiss, then later an American, citizen. In 1905, he advanced his special theory of relativity. By 1916, he had included other concepts to formulate his general theory of relativity. He revolutionized scientific thinking with his ideas about time, space, mass, light, motion, and gravitation, and was one of the founders of the atomic age.

Einstein's renowned equation, $E = mc^2$, stated that matter and energy are interchangeable. $E = mc^2$ means energy = mass (or matter) × the velocity of light, squared.

Einstein contributed to quantum theory in his work with light. Until the end of his life, he worked to prove his unified field theory, which combined gravitational and electromagnetic equations in a single theory.

electromagnetic force. One of the four known *forces* in physics, dealing with the relationship between electricity and magnetism.

electron. An elementary particle of electricity with a negative charge, one of the basic components of an *atom,* and so of all matter.

element. A *member* of a *set* or collection.

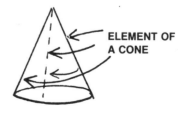

ELEMENTS OF THE SET

In geometry, imagine a moving line segment that *generates* a conical or a cylindrical surface. The line segment at any position is called an *element.* In chem-

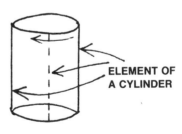

ELEMENT OF
A CYLINDER

ELEMENT OF
A CONE

istry and physics, an *element* is a substance that cannot be separated chemically into simpler substances.

elementary algebra. See *algebra.*

Elements, The. *Euclid*'s most famous work, consisting of thirteen books, which organized what was known about geometry until his time and that also contained chapters on geometrical algebra and number theory. For more than two thousand years, translations of some books of *The Elements* were used as school textbooks.

elements of geometry. The fundamental *assumptions* and *undefined terms.* See *Euclid.*

elevation, angle of. The measure of $\angle$ ABC in the diagram.

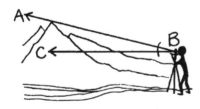

ellipse. A geometrical figure similar to a flattened circle. One of the *conic sections,* an

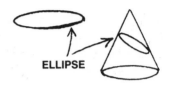

ELLIPSE

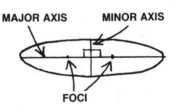

MAJOR AXIS   MINOR AXIS

FOCI

ellipse has two *foci.* The longer segment that passes through the foci is called the *major axis.* The minor axis is a line segment at right angles to the major axis. See *table of formulas, p. 240.*

elliptical geometry. A branch of *non-Euclidean geometry.*

empty set. A set with no elements, written { } or o. A *set* of this kind would be a set of the people now living who are over 20 feet tall.

enclose. To put inside, usually in *brackets* or *parentheses,* to show that an operation should be performed first or that the quantity enclosed should be thought of as one number.

$3 \times 4 + 2$ means $(3 \times 4) + 2$

endpoints. Points at the ends of a *line segment.*

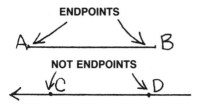

epsilon. The fifth letter of the Greek alphabet, written E or ϵ and used by the Greeks as their numeral 5. In *set notation,* ϵ indicates an element belonging to a set. For example, a ϵ A means that a is an element of set A.

equality. The idea expressed by the equal sign, written $=$. In $4+3=7$, "$4+3$" and "7" name the same number. Three *properties* of equality are:
1. Equality is *reflexive,* $a=a$.
2. Equality is *symmetric.* If $a=b$, then $b=a$.
3. Equality is *transitive.* If $a=b$ and $b=c$, then $a=c$.

equal sets. Two sets with exactly the same *elements,* regardless of the order in which the elements appear.

If set A = {0, 1, 2, 3} and
B = {1, 2, 0, 3}, then
A = B.

equal sign. See *equality.*

equation. A *mathematical sentence* with an $=$ sign between two expressions that name the same number. $6+x=10$ is an equation. So are $3+4=7$ and $a+b=b+a$.

equation, members of an. The *expressions* in an equation on either side of the $=$ sign. See *linear equation, quadratic equation.*

LEFT MEMBER　　RIGHT MEMBER

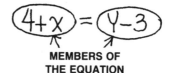

MEMBERS OF
THE EQUATION

equation, roots of an. The values of a *variable* that change the equation into a true statement are called the *roots* or *solutions* to the equation. The root of $6+x=10$ is 4 because $6+4=10$ is a true statement. The *solution set* of an equation contains all the roots of the equation and no other numbers.

equator. The imaginary *great circle* of the earth or any celestial body *perpendicular* to the axis of its rotation.

equiangular. A *polygon* whose angles have the same measure. An *equilateral triangle* is equiangular.

equidistant. Points that are the same distance from a point of reference.

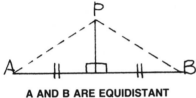

A AND B ARE EQUIDISTANT FROM POINT P

equilateral triangle. A triangle with three sides of the same length.

equity. The value of property, above any charges against it.

equivalent. Two things having the same value.

equivalent equations. Two or more *equations* are equivalent or equal if they have the same *solution set*. $7x - 2 = 19$, $7x = 21$, and $x = 3$ are equivalent equations. The solution in each case is 3.

equivalent sets. Two *sets* are equivalent if they can be

$$\{ A, B, C, D \ldots Z \}$$
$$\{ 1, 2, 3, 4 \ldots 26 \}$$

placed in a *one-to-one correspondence*. For example, there is a one-to-one correspondence between the twenty-six letters of the alphabet and the counting numbers $1-26$.

Eratosthenes (eh-ra-TOS-then-eez), $275-195$ B.C. A Greek scholar, head of the library at Alexandria. He wrote on mathematics, astronomy, geography, philosophy, and the arts. He devised the *sieve of Eratosthenes,* a way of finding *prime numbers*. He evolved a system of chronology, drew a map of the known world, and made an amazingly accurate measurement of the circumference of the earth, given the time in which he lived.

erg. A unit of work, equal to 1 *dyne* of force acting through 1 *centimeter* of distance.

error. Usually used in *statistics* to show the difference between the true value of a quantity and an uncontrolled variation, such as sampling errors.

error of measurement. The difference between *true length* and *measured length,* because no measurement is exact.

Escher, Maurits C., 1902–1972. A Dutch artist whose drawings were based on mathematical principles of symmetry, pattern, paradox, and illusion. Many used strange loops that take the viewer back to a starting point. See *Möbius strip.*

estimation. A number that is not exact but has been rounded off to a prescribed decimal place. Since no measurement is exact, all units of measure are considered approximations. An approximation of π is 3.14. An estimation is also used in another sense, too. We estimate solutions to see whether our final answers make sense. See *error of measurement.*

Euclid (yoo-KLID), about 300 B.C. A Greek mathematician famous for his *Elements,* a collection of theorems and

problems that forms a logical system of geometry. Euclid also wrote on conic sections, optics, algebra, and numbers. He proved that the number of primes is infinite and that $\sqrt{2}$ is an irrational number. He founded the first school of mathematics at Alexandria. For more than 2,000 years, *Euclidean geometry* was the only kind of geometry taught in schools.

Euclidean algorithm. A method for finding the *greatest common factor* of two numbers. The larger number is divided by the smaller one, and the division is repeated, using the remainder as the divisor, until the remainder is zero.

Euclidean construction. A geometric construction made with *compass* and *straightedge*.

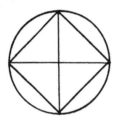

EUCLIDEAN CONSTRUCTION OF A SQUARE

Euclidean geometry. The geometry based on Euclid's *axioms*. See *geometry*.

Euclidean plane. The *set* of all points on a flat surface. The *plane* extends *infinitely* in all directions and so has no dimensions. It is a *subset* of all the points in space.

Euclidean tools. *Compass* and *straightedge*.

Euclid's fifth or parallel postulate. Through a given *point* outside a straight *line,* one and only one straight line may be drawn that is *parallel* to the given line. Questioning this assumption led to *non-Euclidean geometry*.

Eudoxus (you-DOX-us), about 408–355 B.C. A Greek astronomer, mathematician, and physician. He calculated the length of the solar year and is supposed to have formulated some parts of the geometry used in *Euclid's* works. He was the first Greek astronomer to explain the movements of the planets in a scientific manner.

Euler (OIL-er), **Leonhard,** 1707–1783. A Swiss mathematician and a founder of higher mathematics. He is especially known for his work on the calculus of variations. He has been called the father of *topology,* and the Eulerian equation and *Euler's formula* are named for him.

Euler circles. The technique created by *Euler* to represent statements in logic, geometry, and algebra by circles. See *Venn diagrams*.

Euler's formula. In *space geometry,* the formula states that the sum of the number of *vertices* and *faces* of a solid is 2 units more than the number of edges: $V + F = E + 2$, where

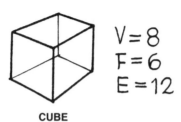

$$V = 8$$
$$F = 6$$
$$E = 12$$

CUBE

V represents the number of vertices, F the number of faces, and E the number of edges.

evaluate. To find the value of. To evaluate $x^3 - 2y + z$, if $x = 2$, $y = 3$, and $z = 5$, the numerical value of the expression is:

$$(2^3) - 2(3) + 5$$
$$8 \ - \ 6 + 5$$
$$2 + 5, \text{ or } 7$$

even number. A number that has 2 as one of its *factors*. If x is any integer, then 2x will be even.

event. In *statistics*, the tossing of a coin is a *simple event*. It is also a *subset* of a *sample space*. See *compound event, independent event, mutually exclusive event*.

evolution. Finding the *root* of a number; the *inverse* of raising to a power. See *involution*.

exact. In arithmetic, exact usually refers to division where the remainder is zero. For example, 5 is an exact divisor of 15. See *approximate; measurement, error of; rounded number*.

existential quantifier. In *logic* and *algebra*, a symbol that means "some." The word "some" means "at least one." The symbol is ∃ and can be written ∃ (x) {2x + 5 = 8}. This is read, "For some x's, 2x + 5 = 8."

expanded notation. A way of writing numerals:

$$3333 = (3 \times 10 \times 10 \times 10) + (3 \times 10 \times 10) + (3 \times 10) + (3 \times 1)$$

3333 is also written in expanded notation as:

$$3 \times 10^3 + 3 \times 10^2 + 3 \times 10 + 3.$$

expanded numeral. A numeral written in *expanded notation*: $200 = (2 \times 10 \times 10)$.

expansion, binomial. The expansion carried out in terms of the *binomial theorem*. For example:

$$(x + y)^2 = x^2 + 2xy + y^2$$
$$\text{and } (x + y)^3 = x^3 \times 3x^2y + 3xy^2 + y^3.$$

expansion of an expression. The product of two or more *polynomials;* the reverse of finding the *factors* of an algebraic expression.

exponent. A short way of writing 10×10 is 10^2. The 2 is called the exponent. 10 is the *base*. The exponent 2 tells us how many times 10 is used as a *factor*. a^3 means $a \times a \times a$. 10^6 means $10 \times 10 \times 10 \times 10 \times 10 \times 10$. y^n means $y \times y \times y \times y$ . . . n times.

expression. A general term for *numerals,* along with signs of *operation, variables,* and combinations of these: 5, $2+6$, x, 5n, $3n^2+6$ and $2(x+3)$ are all expressions. See *algebraic expression, equivalent.*

exterior angle. An angle formed by lengthening one side of a *polygon* to form a side of the angle and using the *adjacent* side of the polygon as the other side of the angle.

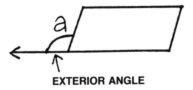

EXTERIOR ANGLE

EXTERIOR ANGLES

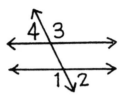

When lines are cut by a *transversal,* the angles 1, 2, 3, and 4 in the diagram are exterior angles.

extracting a square root (or finding a root). To find a square root of a number such as 25 means finding a number that, when raised to the *second power* (or multiplied by itself), gives 25. Since $25 = 5^2$, 5 is a square root of 25. We write $\sqrt{25} = 5$. The $\sqrt{}$ symbol calls for the principal square root.

extraneous roots. In the algebraic process used in solving *equations,* a number obtained that does not satisfy the original equation. Extraneous roots are not correct solutions for the original equation.

extremes. In a *proportion,* the first and fourth *terms.* If $2:3 = 6:9$, then the numbers 2 and 9 are the extremes. See *means.*

F

F. The capital letter F is the abbreviation for *Fahrenheit.*

f. The lowercase letter f is used to designate a *function.* f(x) designates the value of the function at the number x. For example, if f(x) = 2x + 1, then at x = 1, f(1) = 2(1) + 1 or 3.

face. A polyhedron, such as a *cube* or a *prism,* is a solid formed by parts of planes, which are called faces of the solid. A cube has six faces.

factor. In 2 × 4 = 8, the 2 and the 4 are called factors of 8. This means that 8 is *divisible* by 2 and 4. Consider the number 36; its factors are 1, 2, 3, 4, 6, 9, 12, 18, and 36. It is divisible by all of these numbers.

$$1)\overline{36} \quad 2)\overline{36} \quad 3)\overline{36}$$
$$4)\overline{36} \quad 6)\overline{36} \quad 9)\overline{36}$$
$$12)\overline{36} \quad 18)\overline{36} \quad 36)\overline{36}$$

FACTORS OF 36

In algebra, 3 and x are factors of 3x. x − y and x + y are factors of $x^2 - y^2$ because (x + y)(x − y) = $x^2 - y^2$. See *common factor, greatest common factor, prime factor.*

factorial. The factorial of a *natural number* is the *product* of that number and all the natural numbers less than it.

The factorial of the natural number 4 is 4 × 3 × 2 × 1 = 24. 4 factorial is written 4!

$$3! = 3 \times 2 \times 1 = 6.$$

factorization, unique. A theorem stating that any *natural number* can be expressed as a product of one and only one set of *prime numbers.* 6 can be expressed as the product of the primes 2 and 3. 2 × 3 = 6.

factor theorem. If an *equation* such as $x^2 - 3x + 2 = 0$ has a *root* or solution of 1, then (x − 1) is a factor of $x^2 - 3x + 2$.

factor tree. A diagram that shows the factors of a given number. The factor tree for 18 looks like this:

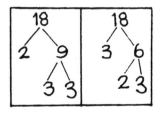

Fahrenheit. A scale of measuring temperature in which the melting point of ice is 32° above zero and the boiling point of water is 212° above zero.

family of lines. A set of lines whose *equations* can be obtained by varying one *element* of a given equation. For example, if $y = 2x + b$, we can obtain a family of parallel lines by allowing b to take on values of integers.

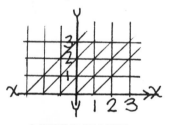

A FAMILY OF LINES

fathom. A nautical measure for water depth, equal to 6 feet.

Fermat (fair-MA), **Pierre de,** 1601–1665. Probably the greatest French mathematician of the seventeenth century. He was a founder of the modern theory of numbers and independently formulated the basis of *analytic geometry*.

Fermat conjecture. *Fermat* conjectured that the *terms* in a *sequence* of numbers having the form $2^{2n} + 1$ are *prime numbers*. *Euler* proved this conjecture incorrect.

Fermat number. A number in the form of $2^{2n} + 1$, where n is a *positive integer*. The first five numbers in this sequence are:

$$5; 17; 257; 65,537;$$
$$4,294,967,297$$

Fermat's last theorem. $x^n + y^n = 2^n$, where n is an *integer* greater than 2, has no solution in *positive integers*. This has never been proved.

Fermi, Enrico, 1901–1954. An Italian physicist who worked in the areas of atomic structure and behavior and the *quantum theory.* He showed that elements could be changed into other elements by bombarding them with *neutrons.*

Ferro (FEH-row), **Scipio,** 1462–1526. An Italian mathematician who found a solution to the *cubic equation* $x^3 + mx = n$, which he might have read in an Arab work. Because mathematical discoveries were kept secret, his solution was unknown until an argument arose between *Tartaglia* and *Cardan* thirty years later.

Feynman (FINE-man), **Richard,** 1918–1988. An American physicist and mathematician who invented, among other things, a way to diagram all the possible histories of atomic particles he was studying so he could predict how they would behave. He said that mathematics was nature's own language.

Fibonacci (fib-o-NOTCH-ee) **numbers.** A *sequence* of numbers, each one being the sum of the two numbers before it. These numbers form a pattern not only in mathematics but in nature. The sequence starts like this: 1, 1, 2, 3, 5, 8, 13, 21, 34, 55, 89, 144 . . . See *Leonardo of Pisa.*

field. A mathematical system that consists of a *set* of *elements,* two *operations* and the eleven *arithmetic laws.*

fifteen puzzle. Invented by Sam Lloyd, a box with movable numbers that can be moved to about ten trillion positions but which have about ten trillion other positions to which they cannot be moved. In the late nineteenth century, this puzzle was played all over Europe for large stakes.

figure. Any *set* of *points* such as *lines, polygons,* and *circles.* In *plane geometry,* a figure is a set of points on a

PLANE FIGURES

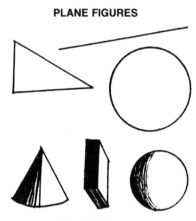

SPACE FIGURES

plane; in *space geometry,* a figure is a set of points in space.

finger symbolism. Most numeration systems are based on either 5, the number of fingers on one hand, or 10, the number on both hands. In some parts of the world, 5 is still represented by an open hand. The Roman symbol V probably started as the symbol for a hand.

finite. Capable of being completely counted; having bounds or limits; the opposite of *infinite.* The set of *natural numbers* from 1 to 10 is a finite set.

finite arithmetic. See *modular arithmetic.*

finite set. A *set* that contains a *finite* or countable number of *elements.* {2, 4, 6, 8, 10} is a finite set of numbers.

five. The name for a number of units whose symbol is 5. 5 is a *cardinal number.* Its *ordinal number* is "5th."

fluid measure. A measure of the volume of liquids. See *table, p. 246.*

focus (pl. *foci). See circle, ellipse.*

FOCUS

foot. A unit of length; 12 inches, or ⅓ of a yard, approximately 30.48 centimeters in the metric system. See *table, p. 248.*

foot-candle. A measure of the brightness of light on a surface.

foot-pound. A unit of work. It is equal to a force of 1 pound moving through a distance of 1 foot.

force. Push or pull applied to a body that changes its form or velocity. There are four known forces in physics: (1) the *electromagnetic force;* (2) *gravity;* (3) the *strong force;* and (4) the *weak force.* The *Grand Unification Theory* in physics proposes that there is one law to govern all these forces. See *string theory*.

force, component of. If we represent a force in a definite direction by *vector* a, we can replace the force with two other forces, b and c. b and c are component forces of a. The triangle we get is called the triangle of force.

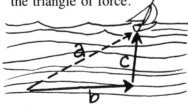

Two or more forces, f_1 and f_2, acting on a body, may

PARALLELOGRAM OF FORCES

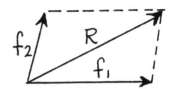

be replaced by a simple *vector resultant* force R, forming a parallelogram of forces. Components of force are used to analyze the forces in terrestrial and celestial mechanics, which is the movement of the earth and the heavenly bodies.

form. An expression of a certain type. The *standard form* of a numeral, such as 347, names the same number as the *expanded form* $300 + 40 + 7$.

The standard form of a linear *equation* is $ax + by + c = 0$.

Form is also a way of stating a principle: $a + b = b + a$ is the generalized form showing the *commutative law*.

The form of an even number can be shown, $2x$.

formalization. Adapting mathematics for a mechanical process. A computer program is a formalized text.

formula. A rule expressed as an *equation*.

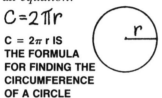

$$C = 2\pi r$$

C = 2π r IS THE FORMULA FOR FINDING THE CIRCUMFERENCE OF A CIRCLE

four-color map problem. Can a *plane* map showing countries with common boundaries be colored with only four colors? If two countries have a common boundary, they must be colored with different colors. For a hundred years no one could prove, mathematically, that four colors were enough. In 1976, mathematicians using high-speed computers proved four colors were enough.

Fourier series. The expression of any periodic function as a sum of *sine* and *cosine* functions.

fractal geometry. A way of looking at patterns from small to larger and larger scale; the way objects and events cluster in space and time; the order in irregularities.

fractals. Tenuous structures built from disorderly growth patterns. Mathematical formulas can produce music or graphic displays on a computer screen.

fraction. Sometimes "fraction" is used to mean a number or a fractional number. Sometimes it is used to name a fractional numeral. The fraction ¾ may be used to show part of a whole. It may indicate division, $3 \div 4$. It may show a ratio of 3 to 4. In ¾, 3 is the *numerator* and 4 is the *denominator*.

Proper fractions have a value less than 1 (¾). Improper fractions have a value equal to 1 (4/4) or greater than 1(5/4).

Fractions such as ¾ and 6/8 are *equivalent* fractions.

A fraction such as ⅝ is said to be in simplest form, or lowest terms, because the numerator and the denominator have no *common factor* except 1.

An expression such as 1½ is called a mixed numeral. See also *continued fraction, decimal fraction, rational number.*

frame. In some texts, a square is used in a number sentence to hold the place for the *numeral,* which is the solution to the *open sentence.*

$$15 - 5 = \square$$

10 IS A SOLUTION

Frege (FRAY-ga), **Gottlob,** 1848–1925. German logician who worked on such basic number ideas as: What is zero? What is number?

frequency. In *statistics,* the number of times an *event* occurs or the number of scores in a range.

frequency array. An arrangement of *data* according to the number of times an event occurs. The data may be shown by a graph or in a column of figures.

frequency distribution. A table showing how often each score, event, or measurement occurred.

frequency polygon. A *broken-line graph* showing the distribution of collected *data.*

frustum (frus-tum). See *pyramid, truncated.*

function. A special set of *ordered pairs.* This table contains a set of ordered pairs {(0, 0), (1, 2), (2, 4), (3, 6), (4, 8)}. The set of numbers

x	0	1	2	3	4
y	0	2	4	6	8

{0, 1, 2, 3, 4} is called the *domain* of the set of ordered pairs. The set {0, 2, 4, 6, 8} is the *range.* If each member of the domain is paired with

DOMAIN {0, 1, 2, 3, 4}

RANGE {0, 2, 4, 6, 8}

one and only one member of the range, the set of ordered number pairs is called a function. To show or describe a function, we may write $y = 2x$; x is a member of the *natural numbers*.

fundamental counting principle. If we can travel from New York to Chicago in 3 ways and from Chicago to San Francisco in 4 ways, then we can go from New York to San Francisco in 3×4, or 12, ways. If a thing can be done in x ways, and a second thing can be done in y ways, then the total number of ways for

doing the two things in succession is x times y ways.

fundamental operations. See *operations*.

fundamental theorem of arithmetic. Every *composite number* greater than 1 can be written as a product of *primes*. For example, $8 = 2 \times 2 \times 2$. Every prime, such as 7 or 11, is its own product of primes.

G

g. Abbreviation for *gravity,* or a unit of the force of gravity. The force of gravity at the earth's surface is 1g.

Galilei, Galileo, 1564–1642. A great Italian astronomer, mathematician, and physicist who laid the foundations for modern experimental science. His construction of an astronomical telescope enlarged our idea of the universe. He formulated many physical laws mathematically, including the first new laws of bodies in motion since *Aristotle*'s. He disproved Aristotle's theory that heavier bodies fall faster than light ones, and developed the formula $d = 16t^2$ for freely falling bodies. He was tried by the Inquisition for supporting the *Copernican* theory of the solar system.

gallon. A unit of *liquid measure,* equal to 4 quarts or 231 cubic inches. See *table, p. 246.*

Galois (gal-WAH), **Evariste,** 1811–1832. A French mathematician who by the time he was seventeen had evolved original concepts on the theory of algebra and had made important contributions to the theories of numbers, equations, and functions. He helped to formulate the theory of groups in algebra. Before age twenty-one, he was killed in a duel.

Galton, Sir Francis, 1822–1911. An English statistician and sociologist, and a cousin of Charles Darwin. His chief studies related to the laws of heredity. He greatly influenced the introduction of statistics to anthropologists and biologists in the United States.

game theory. Sometimes called "Monte Carlo methods." A branch of mathematics concerned, among other things, with *probability.* The term was first used by *John von Neumann* in 1928 to describe the strategy of winning at poker. It was later enlarged to include subjects from military tactics to criminal detection. Computers using mathematics make it possible to solve similar problems in every field of human endeavor.

gamma. The third letter of the Greek alphabet, used for the numeral 3 and written Γ

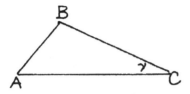

or γ. It may be used to designate an *interior angle* of a triangle.

Gauss (GOUSE), **Karl Friedrich,** 1777–1855. A German mathematician and astronomer, considered one of the most original mathematicians who ever lived. He completed his first major work at nineteen and was famous for his contributions to number theory, geometry, and astronomy. He was the first to prove

the fundamental theory of algebra and was a pioneer in *non-Euclidean geometry, statistics,* and *probability,* the theory of functions, and the geometry of curved surfaces. He invented a telegraph and made a surveyor's instrument.

gauss. Named after Karl *Gauss.* A unit to measure the strength of a magnetic field.

generalization. See *abstraction.*

generate. In mathematics, to trace out. Line AB, moving parallel to line CD, generates a *surface.* The moving line AB is called a generatrix. To

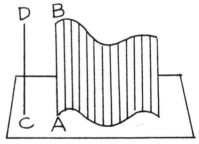

generate also means to form the *positive integers* after number one. For example, $1 = 1$, $2 = 1 + 1$, $3 = 2 + 1 = 1 + 1 + 1$.

Each larger integer is generated by adding one to the previous integer.

geodesic (gee-oh-DEEZ-ik). The shortest line segment between two points in space.

GEODESICS

geodesy (gee-ODD-eh-see). A branch of applied mathematics in which, by observation and measurement, the exact position of points, shapes, and areas of the earth's surface are determined. It is also used to determine the shape, size, curve, and gravity of the earth.

geometric means. The *terms* between two given terms in a *geometric progression*.

geometric progression, or geometric sequence. A *sequence* in which the *ratio* of each term and the one before it is the same throughout. In the progression 2, 6, 18, and 54, each term is three times greater than the one before it. The constant factor, 3, is

sometimes called the *common ratio* of the progression.

geometry. The branch of mathematics that deals with the relationships, properties, and measurements of *solids, surfaces, lines,* and *angles*. It also considers spatial relationships, the theory of *space,* and *figures* in space. The name comes from Greek words meaning "land" and "to measure." Geometry was first used by the Egyptians to measure land and was later more fully developed by the great Greek mathematicians. After *Euclid* organized all the geometry known to his time, very little was added until *Descartes* invented *analytic geometry* in 1637. In the nineteenth century, new kinds of geometry, called *non-Euclidean* geometries, were created. Five kinds of geometry, classified by *Klein,* are Euclidean, affine, projective, topology, and point-set.

geometry, analytic. A geometry that unifies algebra and geometry. Numbers of algebra are attached to the points of geometry. Many kinds of lines, curves, and surfaces then

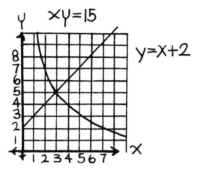

ANY EQUATION CAN BE PICTURED IN A GRAPH

may be examined by means of mathematical *equations.* These equations are pictured in the form of graphs. *Descartes* and *Fermat* were the founders of analytic geometry.

geometry, Euclidean. The geometry based on the *assumptions* of *Euclid* and dealing with the study of *plane* and *solid* or *space geometry.*

geometry, fractal. See *fractal geometry.*

geometry, non-Euclidean. Any geometry not based upon *Euclid's* assumptions; in particular, the substitution of a postulate different from *Euclid's parallel postulate,* which said that one and only one line can be drawn through a point outside a line and parallel to the line. Until the nineteenth century, this was accepted as a "self-evident truth." The replacement of this postulate and the development of new geometries led to a new look at the basic assumptions on which mathematics is built. If we assume that two or more lines can be drawn through point P and always intersect, we have a non-Euclidean geometry called spherical geometry.

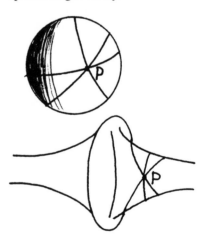

If we assume that two or more lines can be drawn through point P and not intersect the original line, we have pseudospherical geometry.

The founders of non-Euclidean geometry were *Gauss, Riemann, Bolyai,* and *Lobachevski,* all of whom investigated the possibilities of changing Euclid's assumption about parallel lines. See *affine, point-set, topology.*

geometry, nonmetric. "No measurement" geometry.

geometry, plane. Deals with *points, line segments,* and *figures* on a plane surface.

geometry, projective. Deals with *properties* and spatial relations of figures as they are projected.

geometry, solid. Now usually called *space geometry.*

geometry, space. The study of a *set* of *points.* Sometimes the term is used for solid geometry and deals with the study of points, lines, and *planes* in space; figures with three *dimensions.*

geometry, transformation. See *transformation geometry.*

Girard, Albert, 1595–1632. A Dutch mathematician whose works contained the earliest use of *brackets* and a geometrical interpretation of the *negative* sign. He gave us the first abbreviations, sin and tan, for sine and tangent.

gnomon (KNOW-mon). A vertical column used as a sundial by the Greeks. It was placed in the middle of three concentric circles so that every two hours the end of its shadow passed from one circle to another.

Also, in arithmetic, a *term* of a certain kind of *arithmetical progression* of integers. In geometry, the part of a *parallelogram* that remains after a similar parallelogram has been taken away from one of its corners.

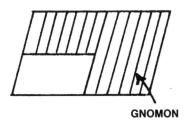

GNOMON

Gödel, Kurt, 1906–1978. A German mathematician known for his "incompleteness theorem." He wrote that mathematical truth exists even if we cannot prove it with our senses.

Goldbach's conjecture.
States that every even number
except 2 is the *sum* of two
prime numbers. Although no
one has yet disproved this, no
one has ever proved it to be
true for all even numbers.

golden section. A *rectangle*
of beautiful proportion, which
occurs in nature and art. The
width and the length, added
together, are related to the
length alone in the same way
that the length is related to
the width. Construct a golden
section rectangle like this:

googol. (GOO-gull) The numeral 1 with a hundred zeros
after it. A googolplex is the
numeral 1 with a googol of
zeros after it.

grain. A unit of weight;
$\frac{1}{7000}$ of a pound or 64.8 milligrams. See *table, p. 244.*

gram. In the *metric system,* a
unit of weight; 100 centigrams or 1,000 milligrams;
approximately the weight of
1 cubic centimeter of water at
4° *Celsius.* See *tables, pp.
248–249.*

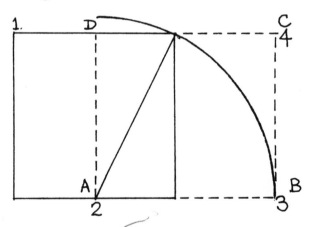

1. DRAW SQUARE

2. COMPASS POINT ON 2, MIDPOINT
   OF A SIDE OF SQUARE

3. PRODUCE LINE WITH COMPASS TO MEET 3

4. COMPLETE RECTANGLE (ABCD)

Grand Unification Theory. A theory in physics that proposes one law to govern all the known *forces*.

graphs. A bar graph is a set of parallel rectangles whose lengths represent quantities for easy comparison.

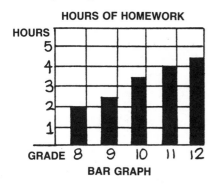

BAR GRAPH

A broken-line graph is a set of points connected by line segments. It is usually used to show a trend.

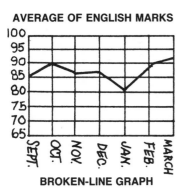

BROKEN-LINE GRAPH

A picture graph, sometimes called a pictograph, uses symbols instead of lines or bars.

NUMBER OF BOOKS PER FAMILY BORROWED FROM LIBRARY

**PICTOGRAPH
(EACH SYMBOL REPRESENTS ONE BOOK)**

A circle graph shows the relationship of all the parts of the whole.

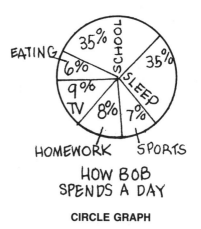

CIRCLE GRAPH

**GRAPH OF A
LINEAR EQUATION**

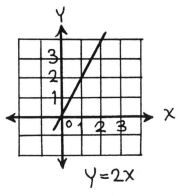

$Y = 2X$

René Descartes, the inventor of *analytic geometry,* found a way to picture *linear equations* in graph form. The graph of an equation is the graph of the *solutions* to the equation.

gravity. One of the four known forces in physics; the force that holds the universe together.

greater than (or more than). A term referring to an *inequality* between numbers. The symbol is $>$ with the point toward the smaller number. $7>6$ means 7 is greater than 6. See *less than.*

greatest common factor or **greatest common divisor.** The largest number that is a *divisor* of a *set* of numbers. For example, the greatest common divisor of 30 and 24 is 6. The greatest common divisor is sometimes written G.C.D. See *Euclidean algorithm.*

greatest possible error. Half of the smallest division on any measuring scale. If a measurement were 1½″, the greatest possible error would be ¼″, because the indicated measure is ½″. The actual length of a measurement of 1½″ is somewhere between 1¼″ and 1¾″. Abbreviated G.P.E.

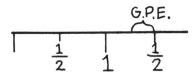

Greeks, mathematics of the. The Greeks were the first to love mathematics for its brevity, and to use it for more than purely practical reasons. They separated it into *mathematica* (pure mathematics) and *arithmetica* (practical mathematics). Many of the great mathematicians worked at Alexandria. *Euclid* wrote his *Elements* and founded the School of Mathematics there. *Hipparchus,* the inventor of *trigonometry,* worked there; so did *Apollonius,* the discoverer of *conic sections. Archimedes* studied there. See *Alexandrian School.*

The Greeks were great geometers. They tried to square the *circle,* double the *cube,* and *trisect* an angle. These are known as the problems of antiquity. All have been proved impossible to solve.

Their numeration system, based on the letters of the Greek alphabet, was awkward. (A little mark next to a letter meant that it was being used as a numeral)

$$\alpha'\ \beta'\ \gamma'\ \varsigma'\ \epsilon'\ \varsigma'\ \varsigma'\ \eta'\ \theta'$$
$$1\ \ 2\ \ 3\ \ 4\ \ 5\ \ 6\ \ 7\ \ 8\ \ 9$$

$$\iota'\ \kappa'\ \lambda'\ \mu'\ \nu'\ \xi'\ o'\ \pi'\ \varphi'$$
$$10\ \ 20\ \ 30\ \ 40\ \ 50\ \ 60\ \ 70\ \ 80\ \ 90$$

$$\rho'\ \sigma'\ \tau'\ \upsilon'\ \phi'$$
$$100\ \ 200\ \ 300\ \ 400\ \ 500$$

$$\chi'\ \psi'\ \omega'\ \overline{\pi}'$$
$$600\ 700\ 800\ 900$$

grid. A grating made by crossing lines at right angles, such as the grid used for making a *graph.*

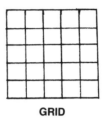

GRID

gross. A collection or set of 144 things; twelve dozen.

gross weight. The weight of a container and its contents.

group. A mathematics system with a *set* of *elements* and one *binary operation* with the following properties:

1. The set is *closed* under the operation.

2. The operation is *associative.*

3. It has an *identity element.*

4. There must be an *inverse element* for every member of the set.

5. If the group has a *commutative property,* it is known as a *commutative group* or Abelian group. See *Abel, Niels.*

The *integers* form a group under addition. Zero is the

identity element and every element, such as -5, has an inverse, such as $+5$. See *field*.

grouping. Arranging things in larger units, as grouping by twos or fives. In the *decimal system* things are grouped into tens (called the *base*). In the *duodecimal system* things are grouped into twelves. In the decimal system, *place value* gives us a way of writing about groups of ten. Usually there is a new way of writing the next larger group.

PLACE VALUE CHART		
HUNDRED	TENS	ONES
2	4	3

243 = 2 GROUPS OF 100
4 GROUPS OF 10
3 GROUPS OF 1

Primitive peoples may have counted sheep individually by pebbles, and then used a larger stone for each group of ten, just as a dime represents our way of grouping ten pennies.

H

h. Abbreviation for *hour* or *height*. h may mean the *line segment* AD or the length of the line segment.

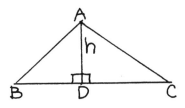

h is also the symbol for *Planck's constant*.

ha. Abbreviation for *hectare*.

half. One of two equal parts into which something is divided.

half-closed interval. The symbol used in [ ). [−1, 3) means all the numbers greater than or equal to −1 and less than 3.

CLOSED END OF INTERVAL   **OPEN END OF INTERVAL**

$$-2 \ -1 \ 0 \ +1 \ +2 \ +3 \ +4$$

HALF-CLOSED INTERVAL

half-line. The *point* of a *line* that separates the line into two half-lines. This point is usu-

ally not considered part of either half-line.

HALF-LINES

half-open interval. The symbol used is ( ]. (−1, 3] means all numbers greater than −1 and less than or equal to 3.

OPEN END   **CLOSED END**

$$-3 \ -2 \ -1 \ 0 \ +1 \ +2 \ +3 \ +4 \ +5$$

HALF-OPEN INTERVAL

half-plane. A line that divides the *plane* into two half-planes. The line is usually not considered part of either half-plane.

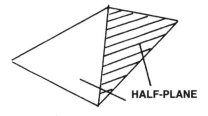

HALF-PLANE

half-space. A *plane* divides *space* into two half-spaces (like cutting a ball into two parts).

Hamilton, Sir William, 1805–1865. An Irish mathematician who made many contributions to the fields of optics and mechanics. His *Elements of Quaternions,* issued in 1886, is said to have been as great an advance over previous *analytic geometry* as analytic geometry was over *Euclidean geometry.*

hardware. The physical *computer* itself and its accessories. The actual equipment, as opposed to the *software,* which consists of programs, or computer instructions.

harmonic mean. The harmonic mean between two numbers is a number whose *reciprocal* is the *arithmetic mean* of the reciprocals of the

RECIPROCAL OF $\quad 3 = \dfrac{1}{3}$

RECIPROCAL OF $\quad 4 = \dfrac{1}{4}$

ARITHMETIC MEAN BETWEEN

$$\dfrac{1}{3} \text{ and } \dfrac{1}{4} = \dfrac{7}{24}$$

HARMONIC MEAN $\dfrac{24}{7}$

numbers. For example, the harmonic mean between 3 and 4 is $\frac{24}{7}$. Usually, a table of reciprocals is used, so figuring is not necessary.

harmonic progression. A sequence of numbers whose *reciprocals* form an *arithmetic progression.* ½, ¼, ⅙, and ⅛ is a harmonic progression because ²⁄₁, ⁴⁄₁, ⁶⁄₁, and ⁸⁄₁ is an arithmetic progression.

Harriot, Thomas, 1560–1621. An English mathematician and astronomer. He was tutor to Sir Walter Raleigh, who sent him to Virginia where he made one of the first large-scale statistical surveys. He made important contributions to *algebra,* introducing new symbols and notations.

heap. A collection of things lying one on another. In ancient Egypt, the symbol for the word "heap" indicated an unknown quantity. The symbol used by *Diophantus* to represent an unknown may have stood for the Greek word for heap.

Hebrew number symbols. These were letters, like Greek

number symbols. See *aleph null.*

hecta. Prefix meaning hundred.

hectare (HECK-tere). In the metric system, 10,000 square meters, or 2.47 acres. See *tables, pp. 248–249.*

hectogram. In the metric system, 100 grams, or about 3.52 ounces in *avoirdupois* weight. See *tables, pp. 248–249.*

hectoliter. In the metric system, 100 liters. See *tables, pp. 248–249.*

hectometer. In the metric system, 100 meters, or about 328 feet. See *tables, pp. 248–249.*

height. See *altitude.*

Heisenberg, Werner Karl, 1901–1976. The German physicist who formulated the uncertainty principle, a principle of *quantum mechanics* which states that two related quantities—such as the speed and the position of a *sub-atomic particle*—cannot both be accurately measured at the same time. If we determine speed, position is uncertain. If we accurately measure position, we cannot observe speed.

helix (HEE-liks). A *spiral;* a curve that lies on a cylinder or cone. It cuts the elements of a figure at a constant angle.

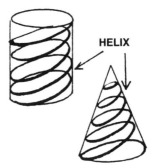

hemisphere. Half of a sphere, bounded by a *great circle.*

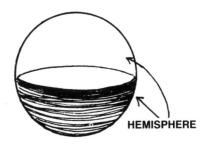

hepta. Prefix meaning seven.

heptagon. A *polygon* having seven sides.

heptahedron. A solid figure with seven faces.

Hertz, Heinrich, 1857–1894. A German physicist who demonstrated the phenomenon of electromagnetic *waves*. He showed that their length and velocity could be measured and that heat and light are electromagnetic waves. The unit of frequency for these waves, the hertz, is named for him.

Hermite (air-MEET), **Charles,** 1822–1901. A French mathematician who made valuable contributions to the theory of numbers, the theory of elliptic functions, and the theory of equations.

Hero of Alexandria (or Heron). A mathematician and inventor who lived some time between the second century B.C. and the third century A.D. He wrote on the measurement of geometric figures and is believed to have found a formula for measuring the area of a triangle when its sides are known. He invented many devices powered by water, steam, or compressed air, including a steam engine.

Hero's formula, named after *Hero,* is a formula for finding the area of a triangle in terms of the lengths of sides a, b, and c.

$$A = \sqrt{s\,(s-a)\,(s-b)\,(s-c)}$$
where $s = \frac{1}{2}\,(a+b+c)$

hexa. Prefix meaning six.

hexagon. A *polygon* having six sides.

hexagram. A geometric figure made by two *equilateral*

HEXAGRAM

triangles, with a *concentric* center and parallel sides.

hexahedron. A *polyhedron* with six faces.

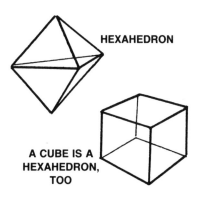

HEXAHEDRON

A CUBE IS A HEXAHEDRON, TOO

Hilbert, David, 1862−1943. A German mathematician who wrote *The Foundations of Geometry,* which established geometry as an abstract study of purely formal character, depending upon a set of *postulates.*

Hindu-Arabic numeration system. The system of sym-

bols and *place value* the Hindus used to express numbers. Our modern system of numerals is derived from it.

0 ? ʒ̣ ʒ̣ 8 ५ ६ ७ ८ ९
0 1 2 3 4 5 6 7 8 9

Hindus, mathematics of. The Hindus, about 1,500 years ago, made the greatest contribution ever to a system for expressing numbers. They used the idea of *place value* and of base ten. The mathematicians of India also wrote and worked with fractions the way we do today. Their mathematics was passed on to us through the Arabs, so we call it the Hindu-Arabic system. See above.

Hipparchus (hip-ARK-us). A second-century B.C. Greek astronomer and mathematician who discussed the procession of the equinoxes, made the first chart of the heavens, and suggested a method of determining longitude. He developed the first system of *trigonometry.*

Hippocrates (hip-POCK-rahteez) **of Chios,** 440 (?) B.C. One of the greatest Greek geometricians. He wrote the first elementary textbook on geometry, which was probably the basis for the geometry of *Euclid*. He is supposed to have been the first to use letters to name points and lines in geometric drawings. He proved many propositions, among them that similar *elements* of a circle contain equal angles. His best-known discoveries were concerned with the *quadrature* of the circle and the duplication of the cube.

histogram. In statistics, a *graph* showing a *frequency distribution*. It is usually drawn on paper laid out in

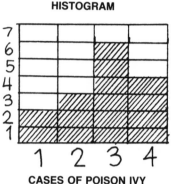

HISTOGRAM

CASES OF POISON IVY DURING 4 WEEKS OF MAY

small rectangles. This is sometimes called a column diagram.

horizontal line. A line parallel to, or on a level with, the horizon.

horizontal change. The difference of the x-*coordinates*. This difference may be expressed as $|x_2 - x_1|$ or Δx.

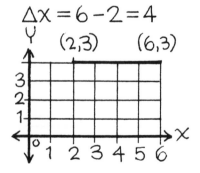

$$\Delta x = 6 - 2 = 4$$

hour. A measure of time, equal to $\frac{1}{24}$ of a day, or 60 minutes.

Huygens (HEY-gens), **Christian,** 1629–1695. A Dutch mathematician and physicist. He improved telescopic lenses, invented the clock pendulum, and developed a wave theory of light.

Hypatia (hy-PAY-sha), c. 370–415. The first woman to take a noteworthy position in mathematics. She presided over the Neoplatonic school at Alexandria and was martyred in 415.

hyperbola (hy-PER-ba-la). See *conic sections.*

hypercomplex numbers. See *quaternions.*

hypercube. An imagined solid with four dimensions. In mathematics this is possible, even in a three-dimensional world.

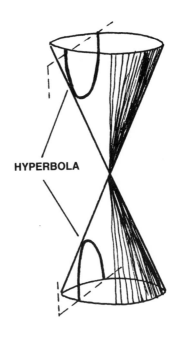

HYPERBOLA

hypotenuse (hy-POT-an-oos). The longest side of a plane right triangle; the side of a plane right triangle opposite the right angle.

hypothesis. A proposition assumed or given as true in order to prove something else.

I

I. The Roman numeral for 1.

i. Designates an *imaginary number* with the property $i^2 = -1$.

icosahedron (eye-COH-sa-HEED-run). A *polyhedron* having twenty faces.

ICOSAHEDRON

identical. The property of being exactly alike. For geometric figures, see *congruent*.

identical sets. See *equal sets*.

identities. Statements of *equality* that are true for all meaningful values of the *variables*. For example, $2y + 4y = 6y$. For any value of y, the statement is true. Used mostly in *trigonometry*.

identity element. The sum of zero and any number is that number. $4 + 0 = 4$. The number 0 is called the *additive identity*. The product of one and any number is that number. $1 \times 7 = 7$. The number 1 is called the *multiplicative identity*.

if . . . then. See *conditional open sentence*.

imaginary number, pure. A *complex number* is of the form $a + bi$ where a and b are *real numbers* and $i^2 = -1$. When $a = 0$ and $b \neq 0$, we have a pure imaginary number.

implication. See *conditional open sentence, hypothesis*.

improper fraction. See *fraction*. The expression "improper fraction" means a fraction whose numerator is larger than or equal to the denominator: $\frac{3}{3}$, $\frac{8}{3}$.

inch. A unit of length; approximately 2.54 centimeters, $\frac{1}{12}$ of a foot. See *tables, pp. 244, and 248–249*.

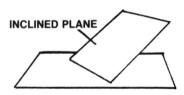

INCLINED PLANE

inclined plane. A *plane oblique* to another horizontal plane.

inclusion symbols. See *braces, brackets, parentheses, table, p. 238.*

$$\{ \quad \}[\quad](\quad)$$

incommensurable line segments. *Line segments* with no common measure.

inconsistent equations. Two *equations* that have no common *solution set:* $y = x + 1$; $y = x + 3$. Their graphs are parallel lines with no point in common.

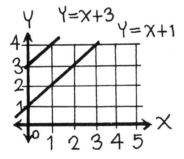

increment (in-KRA-ment). An amount added to or subtracted from a value of a *variable*. If x is a variable, Δx usually represents a small increment.

incurvate. Curving, usually inward.

independent equations. Two *consistent equations* having only one solution in common, such as $x - y = 3$, $x + y = 7$.

independent event. When the outcome of one event has nothing to do with the outcome of another event, they are said to be independent events. If you toss a coin and it comes up heads, there is still a 50–50 chance that it will come up heads on the next toss. Each toss is an independent event.

independent variable. In an *ordered pair,* (x, y), x may be the independent variable. The values assigned to y depend on the values given to x. Thus, y is the *dependent variable.* See *function.*

indeterminate equation. An *equation* containing more than one *variable,* such as $5x + 6y = 9$.

index (pl. *indices*). In $\sqrt[3]{8}$ the index is 3. If no index is indicated, as in $\sqrt{4}$, the index is 2.

index number. In *statistics,* a number used to compare some quantity, such as cost of living at different times. If the cost of living index is set at 100 based on 1966–67 prices, and if it reaches 120 in 1989, one can see how much it has gone up.

India, mathematics of. See *Hindu-Arabic numeration system; Hindus, mathematics of.*

indirect measurement. It may be impossible to measure a particular distance directly with a measuring instrument. However, if other measurements can be made and a formula used, the particular distance is said to be found indirectly.

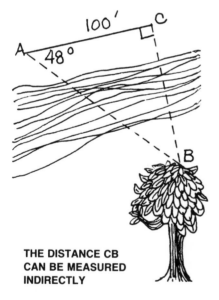

THE DISTANCE CB CAN BE MEASURED INDIRECTLY

induction, mathematical. A method for proving a proposition. A proposition holds true for the first case when tested. Assume the proposition is true for the *n*th case. Check the proposition for the next case after *n*. If this case is true, then we say the proposition is true for all cases.

inequality. A sentence stating that one quantity is greater than ($>$), less than ($<$), or not equal to ($\neq$) another quantity:

$$3x > 4$$
$$x < 5$$
$$x \neq 0$$

infinite. Not *finite* or countable, endless.

infinite sequence. A *set* of *elements* in *one-to-one correspondence* with the *natural numbers;* for example, 2, 4, 6, 8, 10 . . . There is no last term in the *sequence.*

infinite series. Any indicated sum of an *infinite set* of terms. For example, $1 + 2 + 3 + 4 + 5$ . . . $+ n +$ . . .

infinite set. A set whose elements cannot be counted because they are unlimited. For example, the set of even numbers is infinite: {2, 4, 6, 8, 10 . . .}. There is no last even number.

infinity. The concept of endlessness, shown by the ∞ symbol; infinity is a concept, not a number.

initial point. See *terminal point.*

input. Data fed into a computer from a keyboard, diskette, magnetic tape, etc.

inscribed angle. An angle whose *vertex* is on the circle and whose sides intersect the circle.

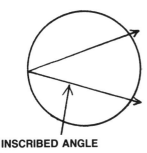

INSCRIBED ANGLE

inscribed circle. A circle inscribed in a *polygon.* Each side of the polygon has only

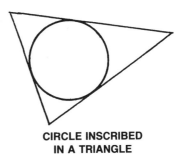

CIRCLE INSCRIBED IN A TRIANGLE

one point in common with the circle.

inscribed polygon. A polygon whose *vertices* are on a circle.

INSCRIBED POLYGON

installment buying. Buying goods for a part of the total price, then paying the balance in equal payments at regular intervals, usually with interest added to the original price.

integer. -3 is an integer. So are -2, -1, 0, $+1$, $+2$, $+3$ . . . Those integers greater than zero are called *positive integers*. Integers less than zero are *negative integers*.

integral calculus. The branch of mathematics that is concerned with finding the *limit* of a *sum* of *terms* and may be used for determining the *area* bounded by a curve or the work done by a force. See *calculus*.

integral domain. A mathematical system. A *set* of *elements* for which two *operations,* addition and multiplication, are defined, so that:

1. $a + b$ and $a \times b$ determine *unique elements* from the set of elements.
2. The *distributive,* two *commutative,* and two *associative properties* are true.
3. The *additive identity* and *multiplicative identity* exist.
4. For each element a, there is an element $-a$, such that $a + (-a) = 0$.
5. If $c \neq 0$ and $ca = cb$, then $a = b$. The set of *integers* is an example of an integral domain.

integral exponents. $4^2 = 16$,

$$4^0 = 1, \quad 4^{-2} = \frac{1}{16}$$

See *exponent, integer*.

intercept. To cut, as a line intercepting a circle. The line

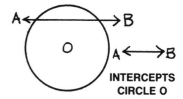

INTERCEPTS
CIRCLE O

$y = x + 3$ intercepts the y-axis at $(0, 3)$. 3 is called the y-intercept. See *x-intercept, y-intercept*.

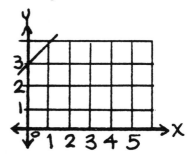

interest. Payment for the use of money borrowed.

interest, compound. See *compound interest*.

interior. The interior of $\angle$ ABC is the *intersection* of two

INTERIOR

half-planes. It does not include the angle.

interior angles. On a *polygon,* the angles in the interior of the polygon. When two or more lines are intersected by a *transversal,* the angles 3, 4, 5, and 6 are interior angles.

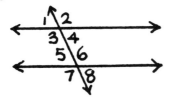

interpolation. A method of finding values between any two known values.

intersection. A *set* of *elements* two given sets have in common is called the intersection of the two sets. The symbol for intersection is ∩, sometimes called *cap.* For example, if set A = {0, 1, 2, 3, 4} and set B = {0, 2, 4, 6},

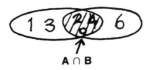

A ∩ B

then the intersection of sets A and B is A ∩ B = {0, 2, 4}.

intersection of lines. Two distinct lines may have at most one point in common. Point A is the intersection of l_1 and l_2. Two *parallel* lines have no point in common. Their intersection is said to be empty.

intersection of planes. The intersection of two *planes* is a line. See *dihedral angle.*

INTERSECTION OF PLANES

intersection of regions of circles. The common *regions* of two or more circles.

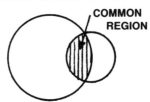

COMMON REGION

interval. A *set* containing all the numbers between two given numbers and the two given numbers, one of them, or neither one. If it is a *closed interval*, it contains the two given numbers and all numbers between them. See *half-closed* or *half-open interval*.

invariant. See *transformation geometry*.

inverse. Opposite. See *additive inverse, multiplicative inverse*.

inverse variation. Some *ordered pairs* are shown in the table. The product of the members of each pair is *con-stant*. (In this table it is 2.) Such a *function* is called an inverse variation. We say y varies inversely as x varies, and write $y = \dfrac{k}{x}$, where x and y are *variables* and k is a constant.

X	Y
1	2
2	1
3	$\frac{2}{3}$

$Y = \dfrac{2}{X}$ OR $XY = 2$

involution. The raising of a quantity to a given *power*.

irrational numbers. *Rational numbers* can be expressed in the form $\dfrac{a}{b}$ where a and b are *integers* and b≠0. Irrational numbers are *real numbers* that are not rational. For example, $\sqrt{2}$ is irrational.

isogonal (eye-SOG-uh-nal). Having equal angles.

isomorphism. A one-to-one correspondence of a set A with a set B. The two sets are said to be isomorphic.

isosceles (eye-SOSS-uh-leez) **triangle.** A triangle in which two sides have the same measure.

J

Jacobi, Carl, 1804–1851. A German mathematician who, like *Abel,* presented a new branch of mathematics called the theory of elliptic functions. His statement "One must always invert" (an operation or procedure) has led to many inventions and scientific discoveries.

join. To unite or add. It is also used to show the *set* made by the *union* of two sets. The "join" of sets A and B (A∪B) consists of the members that belong either to A or to B or to both:

$$\text{If set } A = \{1, 2, 3, 4, 5\}$$
$$\text{and set } B = \{4, 5, 6, 7\}$$
$$A \cup B = \{1, 2, 3, 4, 5, 6, 7\}$$

Join, in geometry, is to connect *points* by straight *line segments.*

Jones, William, 1675–1749. An English writer. The first person to use π to represent the ratio of the circumference to the diameter of a circle. He did this in 1706. However, it was only after *Euler* used it in 1737 that the symbol π came into more general use. π is equal to approximately 3.14 or $\frac{22}{7}$. See *Ludolphian number.*

Jordan's theorem. In *topology,* one of the theorems presented by the French mathematician Camille Jordan (1838–1922). It states: Every *closed curve* in the plane that does not cross itself divides the plane into an inside and an outside. Strange as it seems, Jordan's proof of the theorem was invalid, and it was Veblen who finally offered a valid proof.

joule (JEWEL). A work unit of 10 million *ergs,* named for James Joule, an English mathematician and physicist who was the first to study the relationship between work and heat.

K

k. Symbol for a *constant*. In general, a *function* described by y = kx is a *direct variation*. k is called the constant of variation.

Kasner, Edward, 1878–1955. An American mathematician best known for his work in higher geometry. He coined the terms (suggested by his nine-year-old nephew) *googol* and googolplex.

Kelvin, Lord (William Thomson), 1824–1907. A British mathematician and physicist who invented the absolute temperature scale, sometimes called the *Kelvin scale*. In 1872, he built the *Kelvin machine,* which was a major contribution to modern calculators.

Kelvin machine. A machine built by Lord *Kelvin,* made of pulleys, weights, and connecting cords, for use in predicting tides. The machine gave a physical measurement that was in proportion to the tide at a given time. It was one of the forerunners of modern *computers.*

Kelvin scale. A very precise standard of temperature measurement, based upon a constant-volume gas pressure thermometer. Zero on the Kelvin scale is $-273°C$.

The Kelvin scale is used to measure color which, as a form of light, is a form of heat, too. A degree Kelvin is a measure of the temperature—and so of the differences—in color. The temperature of noontime summer sunlight is about 6,000° Kelvin.

Kepler, Johannes, 1571–1630. A German mathematician and one of the founders of modern astronomy. His three laws of planetary motion state that:

1. The orbit of each planet is an *ellipse,* with the center of the sun as one of the *foci.*

2. The imaginary line joining the center of each planet with the center of the sun moves over equal areas of the ellipse in equal periods of time.

3. The time each planet takes to complete its journey around the sun is proportional to the *cube* of its *mean* distance from the sun.

Kepler, with *Desargues* and *Galileo,* was a connecting link between the mathematics of the Renaissance and the mathematics of modern times. He prepared the way for *Cavalieri, Leibniz,* and *Newton.*

kev. A unit of energy, equivalent to 1,000 electron volts.

kilo. A prefix meaning one thousand.

kilocycle. A unit of the frequency of electromagnetic waves, equal to 1,000 cycles.

kilogram. The metric unit of mass. It is the mass of a special platinum-iridium cylinder and approximately 2.2 pounds. See *tables, pp. 248–249.*

kiloliter. In the metric system, a unit of *volume,* equal to 1,000 liters. See *table, p. 248.*

kilometer. In the metric system, 1,000 meters, a measure of distance equal to approximately .62 mile or 3,280 feet, 10 inches. See *table, p. 248.*

kilowatt. A measure of electric power, 1,000 watts.

Klein, Felix, 1849–1925. A German mathematician who made many contributions to *topology.* He is noted for his work in the theory of *functions* and in *geometry.* He codified diverse forms of geometry. He claimed that geometries were investigations of properties of geometric figures that do not change under certain transformations such as *rotation.*

THE KLEIN BOTTLE WAS INVENTED BY FELIX KLEIN

Klein bottle. A *manifold* in *topology* that looks like a bottle but has no insides or out-sides and is a one-sided sur-face.

knot. A speed of 1 *nautical mile*, approximately 6,080.2 feet per hour. If a ship travels at the rate of 24 knots (never stated as 24 knots per hour), it is moving at the rate of 24 nautical miles per hour. See *table, p. 247.*

koch (coke) **curves.** See *pathological curves.*

Königsberg (KERN-igs-burg) **Bridge problem.** A problem formulated by Leonhard *Eu-ler,* that was one of the be-ginning steps of *topology.* The city of Königsberg had seven bridges, as illustrated, and the problem was to see whether a person could start anywhere

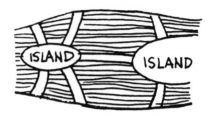

and cross each bridge without crossing any one of them twice. (Euler proved that it was impossible.)

Kowalewski (koh-va-LEV-ski), **Sonya,** 1850–1891. A Russian mathematician and one of the most famous fe-male mathematicians of all time. She was a friend and pupil of *Weierstrass.* Her work with *infinite series* made pos-sible the discoveries of *Ein-stein* and other atomic physi-cists.

L

L. The Roman numeral for fifty.

l. Symbol for *liter*.

A line may be named line **l.**

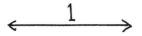

l is also used as a *variable* in such formulas as $A = lw$.

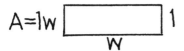

label. Triangle ABC is labeled: $\triangle ABC$.

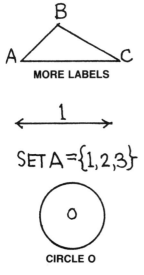

MORE LABELS

Lagrange, Joseph Louis, 1736–1813. A French mathematician, sometimes called the most outstanding of the eighteenth century. He was the head of the Committee on Weights and Measures, which adopted the *metric system,* used by many countries today. He extended the abilities of calculus, solved some of the problems of *Fermat,* wrote papers that led to many of the later contributions of *Laplace* and other mathematicians, and played an important part in verifying the theory of gravitation stated by *Newton.* Besides his work in pure mathematics, he also wrote on mechanics and astronomy.

Laplace, Pierre Simon de, 1749–1827. A French mathematician who, with *Bernoulli,* was one of the originators of the field of *probability.* With *Legendre* and *Gauss* he evolved the theory of least squares. Some of his work opened important developments in hydrodynamics, electricity, and the study of gravitation. Perhaps his most important book dealt with celestial mechanics and

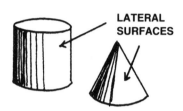

LATERAL SURFACES

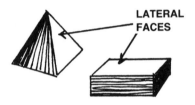

LATERAL FACES

gave an analytical discussion of the solar system, including the methods for calculating the motions of the planets and the tides.

larger than. See *greater than*.

lateral. A word meaning "side."

lateral area. In a *prism*, the sum of the areas of the *faces* or surfaces.

lateral surface. The curved surface of a figure such as a *cylinder* or a *cone*. The lateral faces of a *pyramid, prism*, etc.

latitude. The number of degrees in an arc of a *meridian* north or south of the equator. Lines (or parallels) of latitude run parallel to the equator, and with lines of *longitude* can locate precisely any point on the earth's surface. They are numbered in degrees of

LINES OF LATITUDE

latitude. 0° is the equator and 90° north and south are the poles.

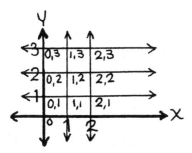

lattice. On this drawing the points (0, 1) (0, 2) (0, 3) (1, 1) (1, 2) (2, 1) (2, 2) (2, 3) are graphed. The lines through the points form a lattice. The points where they intersect are called lattice points.

laws. See *operations, properties, arithmetic laws.*

L.C.D. See *least common denominator.*

L.C.M. See *least common multiple.*

least common denominator. (Also called *least common multiple.*) The least common multiple of the *denominators* of two or more fractions. The least common denominator of ⅚, ¾, and ½ is 12, because 12 is the lowest number into which 6, 4, and 2 can be divided.

least common multiple. The least common multiple of a set of *counting numbers* is the smallest counting number that is divisible by each of the numbers in the set. Some *multiples* of 6 are: 6, 12, 18, 24, 30, . . . Some multiples of 4 are: 4, 8, 12, 16, 20, 24, . . .

Notice that 12 and 24 are common multiples of 6 and 4. The least common multiple of 6 and 4 is 12.

ledger. In bookkeeping, an *account* book.

left. Opposite of *right.* It is usually used in discussing *negative numbers,* or those numbers associated with points to the left of the zero on the *number line.*

POINTS TO THE LEFT OF 0 POINT

Legendre (luh-JAHN-druh), **Adrien-Marie,** 1752–1833. A French mathematician whose simplification of the geometry of *Euclid* is still in use today. He made many contributions to the fields of calculus, geometry, and physics. *Laplace,* because he was jealous, used his influence to keep Legendre from gaining public recognition.

legs of a triangle. The sides of a right triangle *perpendicular* to each other. They have a common *vertex* and are *adjacent* to the right angle.

Leibniz (or Leibnitz), Baron Gottfried Wilhelm von, 1646–1716. A famous German

mathematician, philosopher, and statesman, who was interested in all phases of knowledge. He invented calculus, the chief advance in mathematics during the first half of the eighteenth century. There is still argument over whether Leibniz knew about the work of *Newton* on calculus or discovered it independently. Through the years the best of the two theories has been combined and the Leibniz system of notation is now used.

lemma. A *theorem* that is a step in the proof of a more complicated theorem.

length of a line segment. The measure of a *line segment.* If the line segment has numbers associated with its *endpoints,* the length of the line segment is the *positive* difference of the numbers associated with its endpoints. The length of line segment AB is $5 - 1$, or 4.

$$\underline{\quad \overset{A}{\cdot} \quad \cdot \quad \cdot \quad \overset{B}{\cdot} \quad}$$
$$0 \quad 1 \quad 2 \quad 3 \quad 4 \quad 5$$

Leonardo of Pisa (also known as Fibonacci), 1175–1230. An

Italian mathematician who was one of the first to introduce *Arabic numerals* into Europe. One of his works, the *Liber Abaci,* shows how to solve various kinds of *equations* and uses letters as geometric symbols. For over two hundred years it was a leading reference in mathematics. Perhaps his best-known contribution is the *sequence* known as *Fibonacci numbers.*

less than (or smaller than). A term referring to an *inequality* between two numbers. The symbol is $<$, with the point toward the smaller number. $6 < 7$ means 6 is less than 7. See *greater than.*

light-year. The distance light travels in one year, 6,000 billion miles. Most of the stars are more than a hundred light-years from earth.

like terms. If *terms* are the same with respect to the *variable(s)* and *exponent(s)* of these variables, we say they are like terms. For example, $3x$ and $-12x$ are like terms; $3ab^2$ and $-7ab^2$ are also like terms.

Lilāvati. See *Bhaskara.*

limit. A concept that deals with the idea of "almost equal to." If we continue to add the fractions below to others in this series, the sum will never reach 2. The limit of the sum is 2. $1 + \frac{1}{2} + \frac{1}{4} + \frac{1}{8} + \frac{1}{16} + \frac{1}{32} + \ldots$ is 2.

line. A particular set of *points.* Lines in geometry extend in two directions without end. In mathematics, unless otherwise stated, lines are always thought to be straight. When drawing a representation of a line, arrows are usually put at the ends to show that lines extend infinitely. See *line segment, ray, concurrent lines, parallel lines.*

linear equation. The *graph* of a first-*degree equation* is a straight line. Such an equation is called a linear equation.

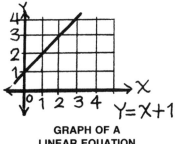

**GRAPH OF A
LINEAR EQUATION**

linear measurement. A measure of line segment lengths or one-dimensional figures.

linear pair of angles. Two angles that are *adjacent* and *supplementary*.

linear perspective. A picture or drawing that gives the illusion of depth.

LINEAR PERSPECTIVE

line graph. See *graph*.

line of sight. An imaginary "line" from the observer to an object.

line segment. The union of two *points* on a *line* and all the points between them. The two points are called the *endpoints* of the line segment. See *ray*.

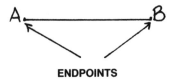

ENDPOINTS

link. See *tables, pp. 245–246.*

liquid measure. See *table, p. 246.*

liter. A unit of *volume* in the metric system; the volume of 1 kilogram of water at 4° Celsius. See *tables, pp. 248–249.*

literal equations. The *formula* that uses letters is the most important kind of literal equation. For example, $I = prt$ and $s = \frac{1}{2} gt^2$ are literal equations. For the second example, we say that the formula (or equation) is solved for s in terms of g, and t. See *table of formulas, p. 240.*

literal numbers. An expression sometimes used to mean a letter denoting any one of a *set* of numbers. For example, n may be used to represent any *whole number*.

list price. The price at which an object is listed in a catalog or other publication.

loan. A sum of money that is borrowed and must be repaid, usually with interest.

Lobachevski (low-bah-CHEV-ski), **Nikolai,** 1793–1856. A Russian mathematician and contemporary of *Bolyai*, who challenged the *parallel postulate* of *Euclid*. He assumed that through a *point* outside a given *line* there are at least two lines *parallel* to the given line. He then constructed a geometry that is now one of the *non-Euclidean geometries*. In this geometry, the sum of the angles of a triangle is not greater than 180°, and the smaller the triangle is in area, the closer to 180° is the sum of the angles.

locus. Any set of points, and only those points, that satisfy a given set of conditions. For example, the locus of points in a plane a given distance from a fixed point in the plane is a circle whose center is the given point.

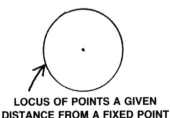

LOCUS OF POINTS A GIVEN DISTANCE FROM A FIXED POINT

locus of an equation. A set of points, and only those points, whose *coordinates* are solutions of an *equation*. For example, the locus of $y = x + 3$ is a line.

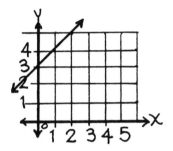

logarithm (LOG-ah-RITH-um). In $10^3 = 1,000$, we call $1,000$ the number, 10 the *base,* and 3 the *exponent.* The logarithm of the number $1,000$ is the exponent 3 to which the base 10 must be raised to give the number $1,000$. Since $10^3 = 1,000$, the logarithm of $1,000$ to the base 10 is the exponent 3.

A logarithm (log) of a number is the exponent to which a base must be raised to produce the number. Log 9 (to the base 3) is 2 because $9 = 3^2$.

Logarithms simplify many long mathematical operations. Where you would have to multiply numbers, the answer can be found by adding logarithms. Tables of logarthims are used to help us find the logarithms of numbers. For example, the log of 427 to base 10 is approximately 2.6304. Thus, $427 = 10^{2.6304}$.

THIS PART OF THE LOGARITHM IS CALLED THE MANTISSA

THIS PART OF THE LOGARITHM IS CALLED THE CHARACTERISTIC

Today, however, hand-held calculators are usually used to do these operations. See *Napier, table of logarithms, pp. 253–254.*

logic, mathematical. *Deductive reasoning* or logic as associated with pure mathematics. *Leibniz* in 1666 used symbols to develop mathematical reasoning. It was further developed by *Boole* and others and is now considered the basis of all new mathematics because its laws can be applied to all mathematics.

MERIDIANS ARE LINES OF LONGITUDE

longitude. The distance east or west of a prime *meridian,* through Greenwich, England. Longitude is computed in degrees, east or west from 0° to 180°. Imaginary lines called meridians, running from pole to pole, connect all places of the same longitude. Meridians cross the equator and the other parallels of *latitude* at right angles. Roughly every 15° of longitude means a one hour difference in time.

long ton. 2,240 pounds, or 20 long hundredweight, a common measure of weight in international shipping. A long ton, also called the metric ton, is equal in weight to 35 cubic feet of seawater and measures a displacement ton.

Displacement is the amount of water any ship displaces. See *table, p. 244.*

lowest common denominator (L.C.D.). See *least common denominator.*

lowest terms. A *fractional numeral* whose *numerator* and *denominator* have 1 as the only common factor. ¾ is in lowest terms or, as it is sometimes called, in simplest form.

Ludolphian (lou-DOLF-ee-un) **number.** Another term for π (pi), which in 1615 was calculated to thirty-five digits by Ludolph van Ceulen, a German (or Dutch) mathematician who worked on the problem most of his life. On his tombstone, π is the only epitaph.

lumen (LOO-men). A measure of the amount of light falling on a surface 1 foot away from a light of 1 candle power.

lux. The unit of illumination or light equal to the amount received at a distance of 1 meter from a standard light source. It is equal to 1 lumen per square meter.

M

M. The Roman numeral for one thousand.

m. Symbol for meter, mile.

Mach (MOCK) **number.** The speed of an object compared to the speed of sound in air, approximately 1,100 feet per second at sea level and at 32°F. Mach 1 is the speed of sound; Mach 2 is twice the speed of sound.

Maclaurin, Colin, 1698–1746. A Scottish mathematician who, in 1740, shared the prize awarded by the French Academy of Sciences with *Bernouilli* and *Euler*. He made contributions to geometry, astronomy, and other branches of mathematics but is remembered chiefly for coming to the defense of *Newton* and calculus and giving geometric proofs for Newton's conclusions.

magic squares. Numbers arranged in a square so that each *row, column,* and *diagonal* adds up to the same total. The earliest known magic square is Chinese and dates back about three thousand years. One of the most famous magic squares was devised by the artist Albrecht Dürer in A.D. 1514 and was part of an engraving called "Melancholia." The square looks like this:

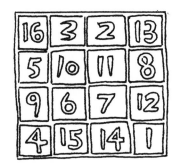

magnetism. The property of attraction possessed by magnets—small ones, such as bar magnets; huge ones, such as the earth.

magnitude. Size. It refers to length and volume.

major. Principal or main, as the *major axis* of an ellipse or the *major arc of a circle.*

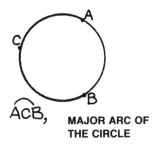

ACB, **MAJOR ARC OF THE CIRCLE**

major arc of a circle. An arc larger than a semicircle.

major axis. The longer *axis* in an *ellipse*.

MAJOR AXIS OF
AN ELLIPSE

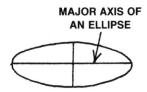

Mandelbrot, Benoit, (1924–). Polish/French/American mathematician who invented *fractal geometry*.

Mandelbrot set. A set whose members are *complex numbers* which can be graphed as points on a complex plane. It is said to be the most complex object in mathematics.

manifold. Another term for space. A collection or set of objects.

mantissa. See *logarithms*.

map-coloring problem. See *four-color map problem*.

mapping. If to each *element* of a *set* there is a corresponding *unique* element from another set, then we say there is a one-to-one mapping of

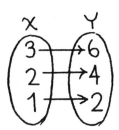

set x onto set y. See *correspondence*.

mapping, many-to-one. A *mapping* in which more than one *member* of one *set* is matched with one member of another set.

FAVORITE COLOR

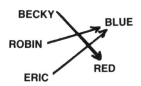

mass. Mass represents the actual amount of matter in an object. It is a measure of a body's tendency to resist a change in *velocity*. If you push a brick, then push an empty shoe box, you will see which has the greater mass. Mass is often roughly associated with weight which is affected by the pull of gravity. Mass is not.

$$\text{SET A} = \{1, 2, 3\}$$

$$\text{SET B} = \{ \text{✏}, \text{📎}, \text{🖊} \}$$

matching. To pair or *associate*, usually in a *one-to-one-correspondence*. See *mapping*.
Set A = {a, b, c}
Set B = {comb, chair, table}

mathematica. The Greek word for pure mathematics, as opposed to practical arithmetic.

mathematical sentence. A sentence that uses numerals, symbols, and sometimes words. It can be true, false, or open. See *compound* and *conditional open sentence, connective*.

TRUE SENTENCE

$$7 > 3$$

FALSE SENTENCE

$$4 + 2 \neq 6 \times 1$$

OPEN SENTENCE

$$2x + 3 = 19$$

mathematical shorthand. A way of writing sentences in mathematics or logic by using *symbols*. For example, we usually think of a formula as mathematical shorthand for some relationship. See *table of symbols, pp. 237–239*.

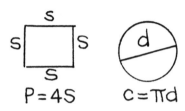

$$P = 4S \qquad C = \pi d$$

mathematics. The study of relations between objects or quantities, organized so that certain facts can be proved or derived from others by using *logic*. It is estimated that there are about three thousand categories of mathematics. Mathematics is a human invention. See *applied mathematics, pure mathematics*.

matrix (pl. *matrices*). A rectangular *array* of *elements*. Mathematical operations are performed on matrices. A matrix might have four numbers or a hundred. Four numbers would be a two-by-two matrix:

. A hundred might be ten-by-ten, or four-by-twenty-five, or any other regular arrangement. Matrices are a way in which complicated mathematical statements can be expressed simply, often through a computer.

Problems in statistics and economics can be expressed in terms of matrices.

Maxwell, James Clerk (CLARK), 1831–1879. A great Scottish mathematician and physicist, the first in a long line of nineteenth- and twentieth-century contributors to modern physics. He won early recognition with mathematical papers and developed the theoretical mathematics of the electromagnetic field. He made enormous contributions to physics not only in electromagnetic fields but in the understanding of light, heat, color, gases, and dynamics. The unit of magnetic flux, or change, is called a maxwell.

Mayan numeration system. The system of the Mayan Indians of Central America. Any number could be written with only 3 kinds of symbols:

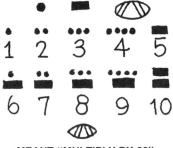

MEANT "MULTIPLY BY 20"

The Mayans had a *place value* system that worked very well.

mean, in statistics. See *central tendency, measures of.*

means, in proportion. In

$$\frac{a}{b} = \frac{c}{d}$$

which can also be written a:b = c:d, the terms b and c are called the means. They are the second and third terms of the proportion. When the means of a proportion are the same, as in $\frac{1}{4} = \frac{4}{16}$, either mean is said to be the mean proportional between the first and fourth terms. See *arithmetic mean, geometric mean, harmonic mean.*

MEANS

a:b = c:d

EXTREMES

measure. To compare to some unit, usually a *standard unit* of measure.

measured length. The measure of an object obtained by

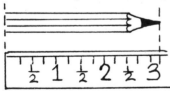

**MEASURED LENGTH
IS 3¼ UNITS**

using a measuring instrument. Because no instrument is absolutely correct, there is always an error of measurement.

median. In *statistics.* See *central tendency, measures of.*

median of a triangle. A *line segment* whose *endpoints* are one *vertex* of a triangle and the midpoint of the side opposite the vertex.

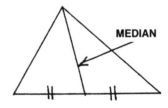

MEDIAN

mega. Prefix meaning one million, as in megacycle.

members of an equation. The *algebraic expressions* on either side of the equals sign. x + y = 8 + 3.

LEFT MEMBER   RIGHT MEMBER

(x + y) = (8+3)

MEMBERS OF AN EQUATION

$$SET\ A = \{6,7,8,9\}$$

MEMBERS OF THE SET

members of a set. The *elements* of a *set*.

Menaechmus (me-NAYK-mus), 375–325 B.C. A Greek mathematician. Pupil of *Eudoxus,* he was the first to discuss *conic sections,* which were called Menaechmian triads. It is said that Menaechmus told Alexander the Great, "There is no royal road in geometry." The same story is told of Euclid and Ptolemy.

Mendel (MEN-del), **Gregor,** 1822–1884. An Austrian priest who showed, by experiments in cross-breeding peas, that certain genetic characteristics are inherited according to the mathematical laws of *probability.*

Menelaus (men-uh-LAY-us), c. A.D. 100. A Greek astronomer and mathematician who lived in Rome and wrote the oldest known work on spherical *trigonometry.*

mensuration. The process of finding the measure of geometric figures; for example, the lengths of line segments, the areas of surfaces, and the volumes of solids.

Méré, Antoine Lombard, Chevalier de. See *de Méré.*

meridian. A *great (imaginary) circle* on the surface of the earth running from pole to pole and cutting the equator at right angles. The prime meridian at Greenwich, England, is 0°. The international *date line* runs roughly along the 180th meridian.

PRIME MERIDIAN

meter. The basic unit of *linear measure* of the *metric system,* approximately 39.37 inches. See *tables, pp. 248–249.*

metric system. A *decimal* system of weights and measures. The standard unit for length is the *meter,* for *mass* the *gram,* and for *capacity* the *liter.*

The metric system was adopted first in France. It is now used for practically all scientific measurements. See *Lagrange; tables, pp. 248–249.*

metric ton. 1,000 kilograms. See *long ton.*

micro. Prefix meaning 1/1,000,000.

midpoint. In a *line segment,* the point that *bisects* the line segment.

mile. A measure of distance, equal to 1,760 yards, 5,280 feet, or approximately 1.6094 kilometers. See *tables, pp. 244, 249.*

mille. The Roman word for thousand and probably the origin of *mile* (which was a thousand paces of a Roman soldier).

milli. Prefix meaning one thousand, or one-thousandth part.

milliard The name given to the numeral 1,000,000,000 in France, Germany and En-gland; in the United States it is called *a billion.*

milligram. One-thousandth of a *gram.*

million. One thousand times one thousand, or 1,000,000.

minim. 1/60 of a fluid dram; the smallest *liquid measure.* See *table, p. 246.*

minuend. The name given to the quantity from which another quantity is to be subtracted. In some of the newer texts, the language of *minuend, subtrahend,* and *difference* is replaced by *sum, addend,* and missing addend.

minor arc of a circle. An *arc* of a circle less than a semi-circle.

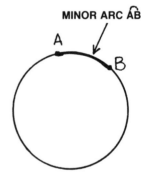

MINOR ARC $\widehat{AB}$

minus. The name for the symbol −. 8 minus 2 is written $8 - 2$ and means that 2 is to be subtracted from 8.

minute. A measure of time, $\frac{1}{60}$ of an hour. A circular measure, $\frac{1}{60}$ of a degree. See *table, p. 247.*

mixed algebraic expressions. The sum of a *polynomial* and a *rational expression*

$$a + \left(\frac{1}{a}\right), \ 1 + \left(\frac{1}{x}\right)$$

are mixed expressions.

mixed number. A term commonly used to refer to a *mixed numeral.*

mixed numeral. A numeral such as $1\frac{1}{2}$, $7\frac{7}{8}$, and $5\frac{3}{8}$. See *fraction.*

Möbius or **Moebius** (MER-bee-us), **August Ferdinand,** 1790–1868. A German astronomer and mathematician; a pupil of *Gauss.* His name is given to a one-sided surface known as the *Möbius strip,* which is studied in *topology.* His works, together with those of *Riemann, Lobachevski, Bolyai,* and others, appeared at about the same time and created a revolution in geometry.

Möbius strip. A surface (invented by *Möbius*) with only one "side." It is made by giving a strip of paper a half-twist and then fastening the ends together. If a line is drawn down the middle of the strip, it will come back to the starting point after having covered both "sides" of the paper, without the pencil being lifted.

TWIST THE STRIP IN ONE PLACE

FASTEN ENDS

mode. Used in *statistics.* See *central tendency, measures of.*

model. In mathematics and other sciences, a structure for testing ideas.

modem. A device that enables computers to communicate with each other through telephone lines.

modulo. See *congruent numbers, base of a numeration system.*

modulus See *congruent*

numbers, base of a numeration system.

Moebius. See *Möbius, August Ferdinand.*

monomial. A monomial can be an *integer:* 7, −3; or a *variable:* x. It can also be the product of an integer and variables: 7x, 5xy, 6(−x) (y).

monotony principle. Same as *addition property of inequalities:*

$$\text{if } a < b$$
$$\text{then } a + c < b + c$$

Monte Carlo methods. See *game theory.*

Montessori rods. Counting sticks used by Countess Maria Montessori, an Italian educator (1870–1952) who believed that children should learn arithmetic using concrete materials. These number rods preceded the *Cuisenaire rods* and *Stern blocks.* Other materials include ten colored blocks, each graded in size and of a different color; oblong blocks for learning measures of *length;* sets of cylinders of varying thicknesses; seeds used to represent *points;* rings for *curves;*

and tablets for *plane surfaces.* The materials are widely used throughout Europe today.

month. A measurement of time, roughly $\frac{1}{12}$ of a solar year. The lengths of different months were arbitrarily set by various Caesars; they vary from 28 to 31 days and have no actual relation to celestial time. A lunar month of approximately 29½ to 30 days is reckoned by the phases of the moon but does not "come out even" with the length of the solar year.

more than. See *greater than.*

Moscow papyrus. Perhaps the oldest existing work on mathematics; one of the chief sources of information concerning Egyptian mathematics. Also called the Golenischev. It is now in Moscow.

multinomial. A mathematical expression consisting of two or more *terms.* The word is currently not in use. See *polynomial.*

multiple. Some multiples of 3 are 3, 6, 9, 12, 15 . . . In arithmetic, a multiple of a number is a number that is the *product* of the given number and another *factor*. 24 is a multiple of 2. $(24 = 2 \times 12)$. It is also a multiple of 3, 4, 6, 8, and other numbers. We say it is a *common multiple* of 2, 3, 4, 6, and 8.

multiplicand. A name given to the number that is being multiplied by another number. It is also called a *factor*.

$$\begin{array}{r} 23 \\ \times\ 5 \\ \hline \end{array}$$

multiplication. A *binary operation* in mathematics. For a pair of *members* of the *set* for which the operation is defined, there is matched a number from the set. For example, to the numbers 3 and 2, there is matched the number 6: $3 \times 2 = 6$. Each number in the pair of numbers is called a *factor,* and the number matched to the pair is called the *product.* In arithmetic, we may think of multiplication of whole numbers in terms of addition. For example, $3 \times 2 = 2 + 2 + 2$. In some newer texts, multiplication is thought of in terms of cross products of sets. Set A has three elements. Set A = {a, b,

**FOR THE SET
OF WHOLE NUMBERS**

$$\{1, 2, 3, 4, 5, 6, 7, 8, 9 ...\}$$

MEMBERS   **ARE MATCHED TO
OF THE SET**   **ANOTHER MEMBER
OF THE SET**

$$2 \cdot 3 = 6$$
FACTORS   **PRODUCT**

c}. Set B has two elements. Set B = {d, e}. The cross

$$SET\ A = \{a, b, c\}$$
$$SET\ B = \{d, e\}$$

product of set A and set B is the set of all the pairs of elements from set A and set B. The cross product has six elements:

$$A \times B$$
1. (a, d)
2. (a, e)
3. (b, d)
4. (b, e)
5. (c, d)
6. (c, e)

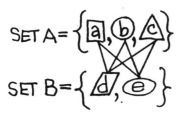

$A \times B = \{(a,\ d)\ (a,\ e)\ (b,\ d)$
$(b,\ e)\ (c,\ d)\ (c,\ e)\}$.
See *arithmetic laws, associative property for multiplication, commutative property for multiplication, cross.*

multiplicative identity. In multiplication, the *identity element* is I because any number multiplied by I gives that number. $27 \times 1 = 27$.

multiplicative inverse. If the product of two numbers is I, either number is called the multiplicative inverse of the other. For example, since $\frac{2}{5} \times \frac{5}{2} = 1$, $\frac{2}{5}$ is the multiplicative inverse of $\frac{5}{2}$ and $\frac{5}{2}$ is the multiplicative inverse of $\frac{2}{5}$.

SET A = $\{4,5,6,7\}$
SET B = $\{0,1,2\}$

**DISJOINT SETS ARE
MUTUALLY EXCLUSIVE**

multiplier. The *term* or quantity used to multiply another term or quantity. Also called *factor.*

mutually exclusive events. *Disjoint sets,* or events that have no elements in common.

myria. Prefix meaning 10,000.

N

n. Used to represent any member in a *set*. For example, for all numbers n, $1n = n$.

It is used in discussing the number of *elements* in a set. The number of elements in set A is 3. This may be written $n\{A\} = 3$.

$$\text{SET A} = \{\square, \bigcirc, \triangle\}$$

nanometer. A unit of length typically used to express *wavelengths* of light.

Napier (NAY-pea-er), **John,** 1550–1617. A Scottish aristocrat who made many contributions to mathematics, chief among them being the invention of *logarithms*. Although it was a Swiss watchmaker, Jobst Bürgi, who first used *exponents* in logarithms, Napier had the revolutionary idea of working out extremely complex tables for multiplication and division, such as are used in astronomy and engineering. After Napier's death, his friend *Briggs* changed the base to 10, called common logarithms, which are much more easily used in arithmetic. But the so-called Napierian base is often used in *calculus*.

Napier was responsible for a multiplication device known as *Napier's bones*, for improving the *abacus*, and for additions to the field of spherical *trigonometry*.

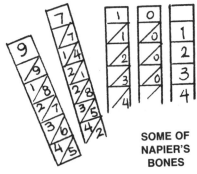

SOME OF NAPIER'S BONES

Napier's bones. Sometimes called Napier's rods. A computing device for quick multiplication, invented by John *Napier*. It was a forerunner of the *slide rule*.

nappe (NAP) **of a cone.** A conical surface (or a pyramidal surface) consists of two nappes separated by the *vertex*. See *cone*.

NAPPES   VERTEX

natural logarithm. Napierian logarithm. See *Napier, John*.

natural numbers. The numbers 1, 2, 3, 4, and so on. Also called *counting numbers*. See *numbers*.

nautical mile. A measure of distance used by ships, approximately 6,080.27 feet, as opposed to 5,280 feet in a land *mile*. See *knot; table, p. 247*.

necessary condition. A logical consequence of a given statement. Suppose we say,

"If a quadrilateral has a pair of parallel sides, it is a parallelogram." It is necessary that a figure have a pair of parallel sides to be a parallelogram.

needle problem. See *Buffon*.

negation of a statement. George Washington was the first president of the United States. The negation of this statement is: It is not true (or it is false) that George Washington was the first president of the United States. The negation of a proposition or statement, p, is often written ~p, and read "not p."

negative numbers. Numbers less than zero. If a is a *positive number,* and $a + b = 0$, b is called a negative number. The negative numbers are the *additive inverses* of the positive numbers. For example, for a positive number $+6$, there is a negative number -6 such that $+6 + (-6) = 0$.

nest of intervals. A *sequence* of *intervals* such that each one is contained in the preceding one. For example, $\frac{1}{3}$ is in the interval between 0 and 1. If that interval is divided into tenths, $\frac{1}{3}$ will lie between .3

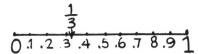

and .4. This interval may be divided again and again. Each interval, lying within the interval used before, has the name "nest."

net. See *development* of a geometric solid figure.

net price. The price of an item after all deductions have been taken for charges, expenses, losses, etc.

net weight. The actual weight of an object without its container. See *gross weight*.

network. In *topology*, the diagram of a problem. See *arcs*.

THE KONIGSBERG BRIDGES
LOOKED LIKE THIS

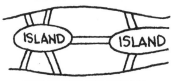

THE NETWORK OF THE
PROBLEM LOOKED LIKE THIS

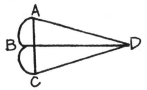

neutron. An elementary particle with no charge, found in the *nucleus* of every *atom* except the hydrogen atom.

Newton, Sir Isaac, 1642–1727. An English mathematician and physicist, sometimes called the greatest genius who ever lived. He formulated three famous laws of motion:

1. A body at rest tends to remain at rest and a body in motion tends to remain in motion (inertia).

2. A change in motion is in proportion to the force causing the change and occurs in the direction in which

the force is moving (momentum).

3. For every action, there is an equal and opposite reaction.

Newton also discovered the universal law of gravitation.

In optics, the study of both light and vision, he demonstrated that white light is a combination of all the other colors.

In pure mathematics, he investigated the *binomial theorem* for negative and fractional values and wrote many papers on algebra and equations.

One of Newton's chief contributions was the invention of *calculus,* which he called the "method of fluxions." For many years argument raged over whether he or *Leibniz* founded this new field. It is now believed that both men worked independently, and although the notation system of Leibniz is preferred, many of the concepts are Newton's.

Nichomachus (nih-KOH-makus), about the first century A.D. A Roman mathematician who published a book on arithmetic that, for a thousand years, was the standard. The book was concerned with the properties of numbers and their ratios. *Boethius,* whose textbook was used widely in the Middle Ages, based his work on that of Nichomachus.

nilpotent An element or *matrix* that has a *power* equal to *zero.* In ordinary arithmetic, zero itself is the only nilpotent element, but this is not always so in other forms of mathematics.

nines, casting out. A way of checking an addition problem by adding the remainders of each *addend* and the remainder of the *sum* when the multiples of 9 are subtracted. The sum of the remainder should be equal to the sum. The final sums must be one-digit numbers.

$$534 \longrightarrow 3$$
$$721 \longrightarrow 1$$
$$\underline{981} \longrightarrow \underline{0}$$
$$2236 \qquad 4$$
$$2+2 = 4$$

nomograph (sometimes called nomogram). A *graph* or diagram, usually consisting of

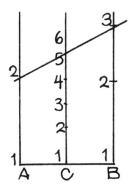

three scales graduated for different *variables,* so that when a line segment connects points on any two, the related value is read where the line intersects the third scale. In the graph, $A + B = C$.

A perpetual calendar is a nomograph. So is a height–weight chart. Engineering nomographs are much more complicated.

nonagon. A nine-sided *polygon.*

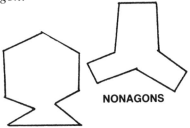

NONAGONS

noncollinear points. If *points* A, B, and C are three points not all on the same *line,* then points A, B, and C are noncollinear. See *collinear.*

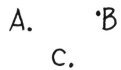

non-Euclidean geometry. See *geometry, non-Euclidean.*

nonnegative numbers. The *set* of *positive numbers* and zero.

nonpositional notation. A *numeration system,* like the *Egyptian,* that does not use *place value* for expressing numbers. For example, ∩∩||| means $10 + 10 + 1 + 1 + 1$ or 23. Each symbol has a value, but the value does not depend on its position in the numeral.

nonpositive numbers. The *set* of *negative numbers* and zero.

nonsimple closed curve. A *closed curve* that crosses itself in at least one place.

norm. In *statistics,* a term meaning normal or average. See *central tendency, measures of.*

normal. In *plane geometry,* being at right angles or *perpendicular.*

normal curve of distribution. See *bell-shaped curve.*

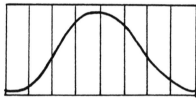

**NORMAL CURVE
OF DISTRIBUTION**

notation, system of. In mathematics, a system of symbols or numerals representing numbers. See *Babylonian, Egyptian, Hindu-Arabic, Mayan numeration system.* Also *binary system, base.*

0,1,2,3,4,5,6,7,8,9
HINDU-ARABIC SYMBOLS

not equal to. 4 is not equal to 5. This may be written $4 \neq 5$.

nucleus. The positively charged mass at the core of an atom, made up of *protons, neutrons* and other particles, held together by the *strong force.*

null set. Empty *set;* one with no *members.* Symbols for the null set are { } and ø.

number. A concept of quantity. There are:

natural numbers,
$\{1, 2, 3, 4, \ldots\}$
whole numbers,
$\{0, 1, 2, 3, 4, \ldots\}$ and
integers,
$\{-3, -2, -0, +1, +2, +3,$
$\ldots\}$
   There is also the *set of rational numbers.* One example is $\frac{4}{5}$. There are sets of other numbers, such as *irrational numbers, real numbers, and complex numbers.*

number frame. A shape used for a *placeholder* in a *number sentence.* See *equation, inequality.*

$$2 + \square = 16$$

NUMBER FRAMES

$$8 < 2 + \triangle$$

number line. A line on which points are associated with numbers in a *one-to-one* correspondence is called a number line. See *zero, positive numbers, negative numbers.*

**PART OF THE
NUMBER LINE**

number sentence. A mathematical *sentence* that expresses a complete thought. Some examples of number sentences are:

$$6+2=8$$
$$6<8$$
$$x=4$$

$$3x+5=17$$
$$6+\square=9$$
$$-5<-1$$
$$3a+a=4a$$

numbers, theory of. A branch of *pure mathematics* concerned generally with the *properties* and relationships of *integers*. In primitive times, and even in the early Greek and Chinese civilizations, numbers were thought to have certain magical properties.

numeral. A symbol or name for a number.

numeration. See *notation, systems of.*

numerator. In $\frac{6}{7}$, 6 is the numerator. See *denominator.*

O

O. The capital letter O is used to name a point as the center of a circle. We say circle O. It is the abbreviation for *origin*.

The letter is also used as a *digit* in the *Hindu-Arabic numeration system*, zero.

o is the numeral for the number of *elements* in the *empty set*.

oblate (OB-late). Flattened. The earth is an oblate *sphere* because it is slightly flattened at both poles.

oblique (ob-LEEK) Slanting; a line that is neither horizontal nor vertical.

oblique angle. Any *acute* or *obtuse angle*, but not a *right angle*.

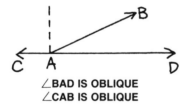

∠BAD IS OBLIQUE
∠CAB IS OBLIQUE

oblique circular cone. A *cone* in which the *axis* is not *perpendicular* to the plane of the base.

oblique circular cylinder. A *cylinder* in which the planes

OBLIQUE
CIRCULAR
CONE

OBLIQUE
CIRCULAR
CYLINDER

of the bases are oblique to elements of the cylinder.

oblique prism. A *prism* in which *lateral* edges are not *perpendicular* to the bases.

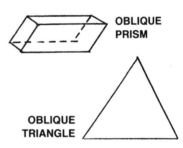

OBLIQUE
PRISM

OBLIQUE
TRIANGLE

oblique triangle. A triangle that does not contain a *right angle*.

obtuse angle. Any angle whose measure is more than 90° and less than 180°.

OBTUSE ANGLE

obtuse triangle. A triangle having one *obtuse angle*.

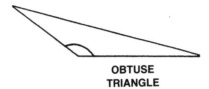

OBTUSE TRIANGLE

occurrence of an event. If you toss a coin and it falls heads, an *event* has occurred. If it falls tails, that is an event, too.

octagon. A *polygon* having eight sides.

octahedron. A *polygon* having eight faces.

OCTAHEDRON

octal numeration system. A *base eight* system. See *notation, system of.*

octant. In plane *geometry,* one-eighth of a circle. In space or spherical geometry, one of

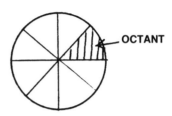

OCTANT

the eight parts into which the *coordinate planes* divide the space.

odd number. Any *natural number* that does not have 2 as a *factor,* or cannot be divided by 2 with 0 remainder. Any odd number can be written $2n + 1$ where n is a whole number. 1, 3, 5, and 7 are the first four odd numbers.

odds. The ratio between the probability of an event occurring and the probability of an event not occurring is called the odds of the event occurring, often stated in terms of "odds against." To throw a 7 with dice, there are six ways in which the event can occur and thirty ways in which it cannot occur. The odds in favor of the event occurring are

$$\frac{6/36}{30/36} = 6/30 = 1/5 \text{ or } 1 \text{ to } 5.$$

ohm. A unit of measure of electric resistance in a wire.

Omar Khayyam, c. 1100. A Persian poet, astronomer, and mathematician. Although he is best known in the Western world for his book of poetry, the *Rubaiyat,* he wrote many works on the geometry of *Euclid,* on algebra, and on astronomy. His *sequence* of *coefficients,* arranged in the form of a triangular number, led to the *probability triangle* of *Pascal.* He is known for his geometric solution of *cubic equations.* See also *Precious Mirror of the Four Elements.*

one. A *cardinal number,* the smallest member of the *set* of *natural numbers* or counting numbers. It is associated with a point that is one unit length to the right of zero on the *number line.*

one-dimensional. Usually refers to a figure having length only, such as a line segment.

one-sided surface. See *Möbius strip, topology.*

one to one correspondence. When every *element* in one *set* can be matched with one and only one element in another set, and every element in the second set can be matched with one and only one element of the first set, there is a one-to-one relationship between the sets.

$$\text{SET A} = \{\triangle, \bigcirc, \textcircled{0}, \times\}$$
$$\text{SET B} = \{1, 2, 3, 4\}$$

open curve. A *curve* in which the *endpoints* do not meet.

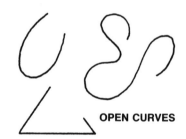

OPEN CURVES

open interval. See *interval.*

OPEN INTERVAL
(NUMBERS GREATER THAN
−1 AND LESS THAN +2)

open sentence. A *mathematical sentence* that includes a *variable* representing any number from a set of numbers. The sentence may be either an *equation* or an *inequality.* $3x + 2 = 18$ is an open sentence. See *placeholder, number frame.*

operation. *Multiplication* and *addition* are *binary operations.* Any *ordered pair* of a *set* is matched with another member of the set. For example, addition matches 5 with (2, 3): $2 + 3 = 5$. Multiplication matches 6 with (2, 3). $2 \times 3 = 6$. *Subtraction* and *division* are not completely defined for the set of *whole numbers.* These operations are not closed or do not have *closure* for the set of whole numbers. For example, under subtraction, the pair of numbers (3, 5) has no number matched with it because the set of whole numbers does not include negative numbers, but (5, 3) has the number 2 matched with it: $5 - 3 = 2$. Division is not closed either.

However, subtraction on the set of *real numbers* (3, 5) has -2 matched with it, and division matches $\frac{3}{5}$ with (3, 5). See *arithmetic operation; intersection, numbers, union.*

opposite. See *additive inverse.*

opposite vertical angles. In the picture, angles 1 and 3 are a pair of opposite vertical angles.

So are angles 3 and 4. This is usually referred to as vertical fours. In *parallelogram* ABCD, $\angle$ A and $\angle$ C are called opposite angles.

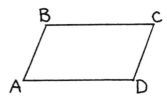

or. A *connective.* A *compound sentence* with ''or'' is called a disjunctive sentence. ''Or'' connects two clauses. ''John is at home or he is at the movies,'' is an example of a disjunctive sentence. It is true if either of its clauses is true or if both of them are true. The symbol for ''or'' used in some books is $\vee$.

ordered pair. Two numbers in a certain order. The pair (3, 5) is not the same as the pair (5, 3). See *Cartesian coordinates.*

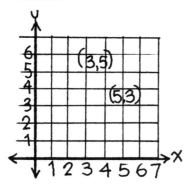

ordering principle. See *comparison property.*

order of operations. Hierarchy of operations by a person or machine, grouping symbols, powers, and roots; multiplication and division; and addition and subtraction, in that order from left to right.

order on a number line. The *point* associated with the smaller number is to the left of the point associated with the larger number. −1 is greater than −3.

order properties of the real numbers. For all real numbers a, b, c, d:
1. If $a < b$, then $a + c < b + c$.
2. If $a > b$ and $c > 0$, then $ac > bc$.
3. If $a < b$ and $b < c$, then $a < c$.
4. If $a > b$ and $c < 0$, then $ac < bc$.
5. Exactly one of the following can be true: $a = b$, or $a < b$, or $a > b$.

ordinal numbers. Numbers that specify order or position of a *member* of a *set.* First, second, and third are ordinal numbers related to the *cardinal* numbers one, two, and three.

ordinate. The second number in an *ordered pair* of coordinates. See *Cartesian coordinates.*

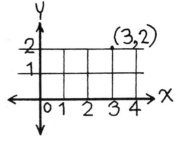

IN (3,2) 2 IS THE ORDINATE
3 IS THE ABSCISSA

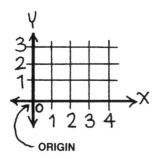

ORIGIN

origin. The point where the *x-axis* and *y-axis* intersect. The *ordered pair* given to the origin is (0,0). See *Cartesian coordinates*.

Oughtred, William, 1575–1660. An English mathematician who introduced the symbol × for multiplication and the symbol : for proportion. He described a circular slide rule in his book *Circles of Proportion,* in 1632 and a year later introduced a rectangular logarithmic *slide rule*.

ounce. A unit of weight; $\frac{1}{16}$ of a pound in *avoirdupois weight,* $\frac{1}{12}$ of a pound in *apothecaries' weight,* ap-

proximately 28.35 *grams.* See *table, p. 244.*

output. The result of processing data in a computer. Can be displayed on a computer screen, stored on magnetic tape or disks, or printed out on a printer.

overhead. Operating expenses in a business, such as rent, taxes, etc.

OVERLAPPING SETS

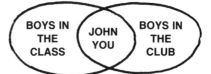

overlapping sets. Two or more *sets* that have one or more *elements* or members in common. For instance, if set A is all the boys in your classroom, and set B is all the boys in your club, and you and John are in both sets, the sets would be overlapping. See *intersection of sets*.

P

P. The capital letter P is used to designate a *point*.

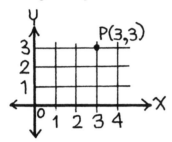

p. The letter that forms the first part of the *conditional open sentence*, "if p then q," written p→q.

Pappus, c. A.D. 300. A geometrician who lived and taught in Alexandria. Some of his work has been lost. Of the eight books known to have existed, the first was probably on arithmetic, the next four were on geometry, the sixth dealt with astronomy, the seventh with analysis and conics, and the eighth with mechanics. He presented many brilliant theorems, but he lived at a time when there was little interest in them.

parabola (pa-RA-boe-la). A curve that can be obtained by cutting a right circular *cone*

PARABOLA

by a *plane* parallel to one of the elements. A parabola may also be described as the *locus*, or path of a point that moves so that it remains equidistant from a fixed point and a fixed line.

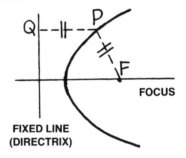

FOCUS

FIXED LINE (DIRECTRIX)

PQ IS ALWAYS EQUAL TO PF FOR ALL POINTS ON THE PARABOLA.

paradox. An argument that appears to show that something that is "obviously" false is true. See *Zeno*.

parallelepiped (pa-ruh-lel-ih-PIE-ped). A *prism* whose bases are *parallelograms*.

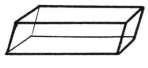

PARALLELEPIPED

parallel lines. Two or more lines in the same *plane* that do not intersect. See *Euclid's fifth postulate; geometry, Euclidean; geometry, non-Euclidean.*

parallelogram. A *quadrilateral* in which both pairs of opposite sides are parallel.

parallel planes. Two *planes* that do not intersect.

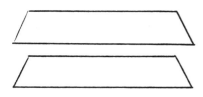

PARALLEL PLANES

parallel postulate. See *Euclid's fifth* or *parallel postulate.*

parallels on maps. Lines of *latitude* that run parallel to the *equator.*

parameter. An arbitrary *constant.* A *variable* in an algebraic expression that temporarily assumes the properties of a constant. For example, in $y = mx + b$, m and b are parameters if either is treated as a constant in a *family of lines.*

parentheses. The grouping symbol ( ). If no rule for the *order of operations* has been agreed upon, $3 \times 2 + 4$ may mean 10 or it may mean 18. When we agree to the rule of first multiplication and then addition, $3 \times 2 + 4 = 10$. If we want addition first we use parentheses and write $3 \times (2 + 4)$, which equals 18.

parity of integers. Two integers have the same parity if they are both odd or both even. Integers are of opposite or different parity if one is odd and the other is even.

particle physics. The study of subatomic particles.

parsec. In measuring celestial bodies, 206,000 astronomical units or 3.26 *light-years.*

partial product. In multiplication:

$$
\begin{array}{r}
235 \\
\times\ 21 \\
\hline
235 \\
470 \\
\hline
4,935
\end{array}
$$

Pascal (pas-KAL), **Blaise,** 1623–1662. A French mathematician, who, at sixteen, was already renowned for his work on *conic sections.* He later became interested in projective geometry, which had been started by *Desargues.* He invented a practical calculating machine that was too expensive to produce. After that, because of a problem sent to him by his friend *de Méré,* he began work on the *probability* theory.

Pascal's triangle. See *probability triangle.*

pathological curves. *Curves* having unusual properties. These are now known as *koch (coke) curves* and are elementary in the study of *fractal geometry.* Among them is the snowflake curve, which can be drawn on a piece of paper but has an *infinite perimeter.* It starts with an *equilateral triangle.* Next, each side is trisected and an equilateral triangle constructed on each. This is repeated.

SNOWFLAKE CURVE

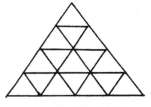

CRISSCROSS CURVE

Another pathological curve is the crisscross curve, which crosses itself at every one of its points. See *Mandelbrot.*

patterning. A *sequence* of numbers in which the same number is added each time. 1, 2, 3, 4 (1 is added). 1, 5, 9, 13 (4 is added). The number added is called the constant, or the *common difference.*

patterns. Mathematics is a study of patterns. Patterns emerge from sets of statements. For example, from this set of statements, is it reasonable to suppose that the product of a positive number and a negative number is negative?

$$(+3)(+3) = +9$$
$$(+3)(+2) = +6$$
$$(+3)(+1) = +3$$
$$(+3)(0)\ \ = \ \ 0$$
$$(+3)(-1) = \ \ ?$$

Peano's five axioms. The five axioms of *positive integers,* as described by Giuseppe Peano, Italian mathematician of the late nineteenth century:

1. There is a positive integer 1.
2. Every positive integer has a *unique* positive integer as its *successor.*
3. No positive integer has 1 as its successor.
4. Distinct positive integers have distinct successors.
5. If a statement holds for the positive integer 1, and if, whenever it holds for a positive integer, it also holds for that integer's successor, then the statement holds for all positive integers.

This last axiom is the famous "principle of mathematical induction."

peck. A measure of capacity, 4 quarts. See *table, p. 244.*

penny. A coin. In the United States, a cent, or $1/100$ of a dollar.

pennyweight. In *Troy weight,* 24 *grains.* See *table, p. 244.*

pentagon. A *polygon* having five sides.

percent. A *ratio* in which the *denominator* is 100. The symbol for percent is %. For example, ¼ is ²⁵/₁₀₀, .25, or 25%. All name the same number.

percentage. A number. 10% of 70 is 7. The percentage is 7, the *base* is 70, and the *rate* is 10%.

percentile. A value that divides the range of a set of data into two parts, such that a given percentage of the measure lies below this value. Thus, if a score of 70 places one in the 80th percentile, 80% of the scores are below 70. The highest possible value for percentile is 99th.

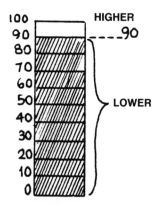

percent of error. The *relative error* of a measurement ex-

pressed as a percent. For example, if we use a ruler scaled in inches, a measurement of 5″ has a greatest possible error of .5″. The relative error is .5/5, or .10. The percent of error is 10%.

perfect number. An *integer* equal to the sum of all its *factors* except the number itself. 6 is a perfect number because $1 + 2 + 3 = 6$.

perfect square. A number or expression that can be stated as the *product* of two equal *factors*. 9 is a perfect square because $9 = 3 \times 3$.

perimeter of a polygon. The sum of the lengths of the sides of the *polygon*.

period. To make reading numerals easier, sets of *digits* are set off by commas. For example, 1,234,567. Each set is called a period. 1 is in the millions period; 234 is in the thousands period; 567 is in the unit period. See *decimal point*. Periods are also used in graphs of the trigonometric functions.

periodic decimals. See *decimals, repeating*.

period of interest. The length of time over which interest is figured. It might be a year, six months, three months, or more or less.

permutation. An arrangement. If there are three books, A, B, and C, they can be arranged in piles of three in six different ways: ABC, ACB, BAC, BCA, CAB, CBA. The order of the ele-

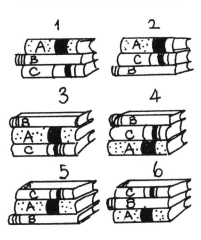

ments is important in permutations. In *combinations,* order is not important. There is only one combination of books A, B, and C.

perpendicular bisector. A line or line segment that is perpendicular to a line seg-

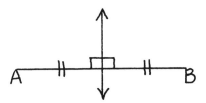

PERPENDICULAR BISECTOR

ment and divides it into two congruent segments.

perpendicular lines. Two lines are perpendicular ($\perp$) to each other if they form two congruent adjacent angles with each other. The congruent adjacent angles are called *right angles.*

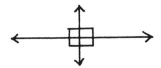

PERPENDICULAR LINES

perpetual calendar. A *nomograph* that tells on one chart the day on which any given date will fall in any year.

physics. The study of all forms of energy and the properties of matter. Physics is dependent upon mathematics.

pi (PIE). An *irrational number* for which the symbol is π. The *ratio* of the *circum-*

ference to the *diameter* of any circle is C/D = π. A rational approximation for π is $^{22}/_7$ or 3.14; carried further, it is 3.14159+. Pi is a *nonterminating, nonrepeating decimal*. See *Ludolphian number*.

pie chart. See *graph*.

pint. A unit of liquid measure; $\frac{1}{2}$ of a *quart*. See *table, p. 246*.

placeholder. A *variable*. In the mathematical sentence, $\square + 3 = 5$, $\square$ is the symbol that holds the place for an element from a given set. If $\square$ holds the place for 2, then $\square + 3 = 5$ becomes $2 + 3 = 5$. In the higher grades, a letter such as x is used instead of $\square$.

place value. In a numeral such as 3,452 written in the *Hindu-Arabic system,* the *digit* 3 represents the number $3 \times 1,000$. The number 1,000 is the place value of the position occupied by the digit 3 in the numeral 3,452. Place values are numbers assigned to positions in a numeral.

Planck, Max Karl Ernst, 1858–1947. A German physicist who won the Nobel Prize in 1918 and is considered the father of *quantum mechanics* with his theory that the basic structure of nature is small, separate "packages" of energy he called quanta.

Planck's constant. A number that never changes and is used to calculate the size of the energy packets (quanta) of frequencies of light. h is the symbol for Planck's constant: $h = 6.63 \times 10^{27}$ erg−seconds.

plane. A flat *surface*. A straight line joining any two points in the surface lies entirely in the surface. The face of a chalk board represents part of a plane. A plane extends infinitely in all directions.

plane figures. Any *set* of *points* in a *plane*. Some common plane figures are angles, triangles, and circles.

plane geometry. See *geometry, plane*.

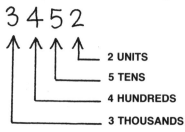

3452

- 2 UNITS
- 5 TENS
- 4 HUNDREDS
- 3 THOUSANDS

plane of symmetry. Two points are *symmetric* to a *plane* if the plane is the *perpendicular bisector* of the line segment joining the points. A geometric figure is symmetric with respect to a plane if for

every point on the figure there is another point so that the two points are symmetric with respect to the plane.

plane region. The interior of a *simple closed curve.* The region usually does not include its boundary.

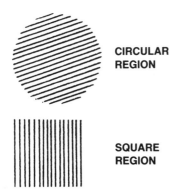

CIRCULAR REGION

SQUARE REGION

planimeter. An instrument, no longer used, for finding the area of a plane figure by guiding a tracing device along its perimeter.

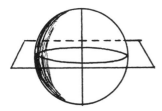

Plato, 429–347 B.C. An Athenian teacher and pupil of Socrates who felt that mathematics was the beginning of all knowledge, as shown in his *Quadrivium.* Like *Pythagoras,* he felt that the secret of the universe was in number and form.

Over the entrance to his school were the words: "Let none ignorant of geometry enter my door." He is thought to have been responsible for the system of definitions, *postulates,* and *axioms* used in constructing geometric proofs.

Platonic solid. See *polyhedron*.

plotting a curve. Locating *points* from *coordinates* and connecting these points with a curve that approximates or resembles the actual curve that pictures the relationship existing between *variables*.

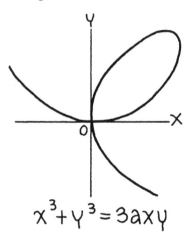

$$x^3 + y^3 = 3axy$$

plumb line. A device made of a string with a weight attached. The force of gravity pulls the string straight down.

The plumb line sometimes refers to the line in which the string hangs and sometimes to the string itself.

plus. The name of the symbol for the operation of addition. The symbol is +.

Poincaré (pwan-kah-RAY), **Jules Henri,** 1854–1912. A French mathematician and physicist who wrote many articles on mathematics. He said that the basis for the choice of *axioms* for a geometry should be convenience and usefulness. He said it was possible to discuss the *properties* of a geometry that could not be "seen" by the senses. He did work in elliptical functions, celestial mechanics, and the calculus of probabilities. His work prepared the way for the revolutionary theories of *Planck* and *Einstein*.

point. An *undefined term* in geometry. It has position but no dimensions and is usually represented by a dot to mark a location. In coordinate geometry, its position is defined by an ordered pair of numbers.

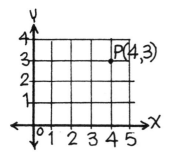

point of tangency. Point of contact. The point at which a *tangent* touches a circle.

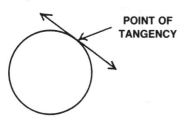

POINT OF TANGENCY

point-set theory. A study of properties preserved under all one-to-one *correspondence*.

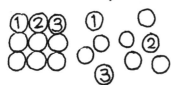

POINTS REMAIN IN ONE-TO-ONE CORRESPONDENCE EVEN THOUGH THEIR ORDER CHANGES

POLYGONS

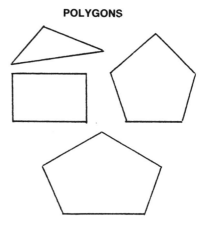

polygon. A simple *closed curve* that is the union of *line segments*.

polyhedral angle. A figure formed by the lateral *faces* of a *polyhedron,* which have a common *vertex*.

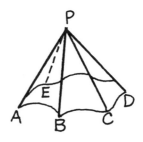

POLYHEDRAL ANGLE P

polyhedron. A solid formed by portions of plane surfaces, which are called the *faces*.

    There are only five regu-

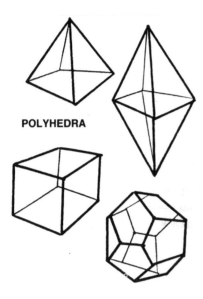

POLYHEDRA

lar polyhedra: regular tetrahedron, cube (hexahedron), octahedron, dodecahedron, and icosahedron. These are known as the Platonic solids.

polynomial. A *monomial* or the algebraic sum of monomials:

$$5y; \quad 6a - 2b;$$
$$2x^2 + 3x + 7$$

$$\frac{3x}{y}; \quad \frac{4(x - y)}{x}$$

polynomial form of numerals. The expanded form of a numeral in which the *place value* of the digits is used: $6352 = 6 \times 10^3 + 3 \times 10^2 + 5 \times 10^1 + 2$. See *expanded notation*.

Poncelet (pon-sil-AY), **Jean Victor,** 1788–1867. A French mathematician. While imprisoned during the French retreat from Moscow, he wrote a famous textbook on modern geometry. He also established the chief properties of conic sections and expanded the theory of polygons. He is best remembered for his theory on the continuity of numbers.

position. See *place value, topology*.

positive error. See *error*.

positive integers. Integers greater than zero. See *Peano's five axioms*.

positive numbers. Numbers associated with points on a number line to the right of the zero point.

possible error. In any measurement, it is ½ of the smallest unit of measure used. If a ruler is marked off in ⅛'s, the *greatest possible error* with this ruler is 1/16″.

postulate. A statement in mathematics that is assumed to be true without proof. Postulates are sometimes called *assumptions* or *axioms*.

postulates of Euclid. See *Euclid.*

pound. A measure of *avoirdupois* weight; 16 ounces. See *tables, pp. 244, 249.*
     A British unit of money.

power. An expression such as 2^3 means $2 \times 2 \times 2$. 2^3 is called a power. It is the third power of 2 and it is equal to 8. In general, a^n is a number and is called the nth power of a. See *exponent.*

Precious Mirror of the Four Elements. A *triangular number* sequence on which the *probability triangle* of *Pascal* was probably based. It was composed about A.D. 1300 by the Chinese mathematician Chu-shi Kei, and is related to the so-called coefficients of *Omar Khayyam.*

precision of measurement. The size of the units determines the precision. The smaller the unit the more precise the measurement. See *true length, measured length.*

premise. A proposition in a proof that leads to a conclusion.

prime factor. A *factor* of a number when the factor itself is a *prime number.*

$$42 = 2 \times 3 \times 7$$

PRIME FACTORS

prime number. A *natural number* greater than 1 that has no other factors except 1 and itself. 2, 3, 5, 7, 11, 13, 17, 19, 23 . . . are prime numbers. (1 is usually not included in the set of prime numbers.) See *sieve of Eratosthenes, composite number.*

principal. The amount of money in a savings account earning a certain rate of *interest.* Also the amount of money borrowed from a lending institution at a certain interest.

principal axis. See *major axis.*

principal square root. Every positive *real number* has two *square roots.* One is positive and the other is negative. The positive square root is called the principal square root. The principal square root is denoted by $\sqrt{}$. The principal square root of 9 is $\sqrt{9}$, or 3.

Principia Mathematica. See *Whitehead, Alfred North.*

principle, mathematical. A rule or law that is either assumed or proved. It may state a relationship between numbers. For example, for all numbers a and b, $a + b = b + a$ is called the *commutative principle* (or property) of addition.

prism. A *polyhedron* with two *congruent* and *parallel faces* called the bases.

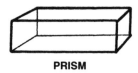

PRISM

probability. A branch of mathematics. If in a single trial, an *event* can occur in s ways, and fail to occur in f ways, and the likelihood of all ways happening is equal, then the probability that the event will occur is $p = \dfrac{s}{(s+f)}$. If in a toss of a coin, heads can occur in one way and fail in one way, the probability that a head will occur in one

trial is $p = \dfrac{1}{(1+1)}$ or ½. The probability of an event ranges from 0 to 1. If the probability of an event occurring is 1, the event is certain. If the probability of an event occurring is 0, the event certainly will not occur.

probability triangle (or Pascal triangle). An *array* in triangle form. The numbers in the array form the *coefficients* of the *expansion* $(a + b)^n$ for n, a whole number. The triangle is used in probability theory. The first six rows look like this:

$$
\begin{array}{c}
1 \\
1 \quad 1 \\
1 \quad 2 \quad 1 \\
1 \quad 3 \quad 3 \quad 1 \\
1 \quad 4 \quad 6 \quad 4 \quad 1 \\
1 \quad 5 \quad 10 \quad 10 \quad 5 \quad 1
\end{array}
$$

proceeds. The amount of money received in a business transaction.

product. The result of a *binary operation* called multiplication of two numbers, or *factors*.

$$2 \times 3 = 6$$

profit. The difference between the cost plus expenses and the sale price of an item.

program. A set of logical rules that gives a *computer* the ability to perform desired operations.

progression. See *arithmetic progression, geometric progression, number sequence*.

project. To transform the *points* of one figure into those of another by any *correspondence* between points. See *geometry, projective*.

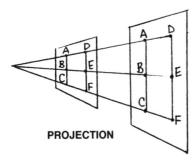

PROJECTION

promissory note. A written statement that is a promise to pay a stated amount of money on a given date.

proof. The logical argument, usually a set of statements and reasons, to establish the truth of a *proposition*. See *conclusion*.

proper fraction. A *fraction* with the numerator smaller than the denominator. ¾ and ⅞ are proper fractions.

proper subset. If every *element* of *set* B is also an element of set A, and there is at least one element in set A that is not in set B, we say that set B is a proper subset of set A. For example, if set A = {a, b, c, d, e}, then a proper subset of A is set B = {a, b, c}. See *subset, complementary set*.

SET A = { 🍒 🍐 🍇 🍐 }
SET B = { 🍎 🍇 🍐 }
B⊂A   **PROPER SUBSET**

property. A characteristic. See *principle, mathematical*.

proportion. A statement of *equality* between two *ratios*. For example, ³⁄₆ = ½; or 3:6 ∷ 1:2, read as 3 is to 6 as

1 is to 2. See *means, extremes*.

proportion, in art. The mathematical relationship between the parts in a painting or sculpture and the actual sizes and relationships of the things themselves. Many artists deliberately distort these relationships to emphasize a point of view. See *golden section*.

proposition. An idea to which "true" or "false" is associated but not both. A *statement* is an expression of a proposition. In geometry a proposition is called a *theorem* when it is proved.

propositions of Euclid. The statements set forth in the *Elements* of Euclid which form the basis for Euclidean geometry. See *Euclid's fifth postulate*.

proton. An elementary particle in the *nucleus* of an *atom,* having a positive charge equal to an *electron* of that atom. The number of protons determines the *atomic number* of an atom of any *element.*

protractor. An instrument used to measure angles.

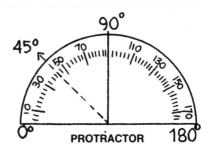

PROTRACTOR

pseudosphere (sue-DOH-sfeer). Invented by *Beltrami* and sometimes called a "double trumpet" surface. The geometry of *Lobachevski* and *Bolyai* was based on the pseudosphere.

PSEUDOSPHERE

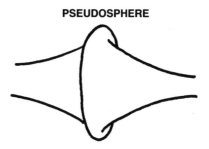

Ptolemy (TOL-eh-mee), c. A.D. 100–168. A Greek mathematician, astronomer, and geographer who was born in Egypt. His work, the *Almagest,* shows that he was a great geometrician. He tried to prove *Euclid's fifth postulate.* His theory of the universe, accepted until the time of *Cop-*

He founded the Pythagorean school. Its members took an oath to keep the teachings secret and hold the same beliefs. Members of the Pythagorean school were concerned with the relationships of whole numbers, which they felt were mystical. Probably the best-known geometric theorem is called the *Pythagorean theorem.*

ernicus and *Galileo,* stated that heavenly bodies revolve around the earth. He gave a value of π as approximately 3.1416.

punch card. An old-fashioned computer card on which certain coded information was written by the piercing of holes in various parts of the card.

pure mathematics. The study of mathematical systems. Pure mathematics does not concern itself with solving practical problems of business or science.

Pythagoras (Pih-THAG-or-us), c. 582–507 B.C. A Greek philosopher and geometrician who said, "All is number."

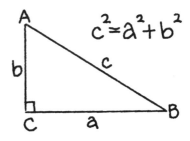

$$c^2 = a^2 + b^2$$

Pythagorean (pih-THAG-or-EE-an) **theorem.** This states that for any right triangle, the square of the length of the hypotenuse is equal to the sum of the square of the length of the sides.

pyramid. A solid figure that has a *polygonal region* for a base and whose lateral faces are triangular regions.

pyramid number. A number in the shape of a pyramid, first discovered by the Greeks, who were interested in the shapes of numbers. The pyramid number is related to a *triangular number* but has

a third dimension, just as a *square number* is related to a cube number.

pyramid, truncated. The portion of a pyramid included between its *base* and any plane section, cutting all the faces except the base. If the cutting plane is parallel to the base, the shape is called a *frustum*.

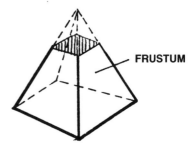

FRUSTUM

Q

q. The letter that follows p in the statement "if p then q," written: p→q. A sentence of the form "if p then q" is called a *conditional;* q is called the *conclusion.*

quadrangle, simple. A plane figure having four points, no three of which are *collinear,* and *line segments* connecting them in order. See *quadrilateral.*

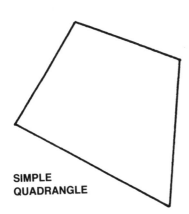

SIMPLE
QUADRANGLE

quadrantal angle. An angle in which the *terminal side* coincides with one of the axes. It is understood that the initial side is on the *x-axis.* The measures of the quandrantal angle are 0°, 90°, 180°, 270°, and so on.

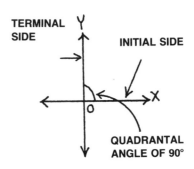

TERMINAL SIDE

INITIAL SIDE

QUADRANTAL ANGLE OF 90°

quadrant of the coordinate plane. The *x-axis* and the *y-axis* divide the *coordinate plane* into four regions, each called a quadrant. The quadrants are numbered counter-clockwise, starting with the upper-right quadrant. Points on the axes are not in the quadrants.

quadratic equation. An *equation* of the second *degree*. Equations of the form $ax^2 + bx + c = 0$, where a, b, and c are *real numbers* and a $\neq 0$, are called quadratic equations.

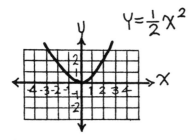

$$Y = \frac{1}{2}X^2$$

GRAPHS OF QUADRATIC EQUATIONS FORM CONIC SECTIONS

quadratic formula. A formula used to compute the *roots* of a *quadratic equation* in the form $ax^2 + bx + c = 0$ and $a \neq 0$. The formula is usually written:

$$x = \frac{-b \pm \sqrt{b^2 - 4ac.}}{2a}$$

quadrature. The process of finding a square equal in area to another given surface, usually a circle or other curved surface. See *circle, squaring the*.

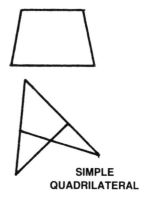

SIMPLE QUADRILATERAL

quadrilateral. A *polygon* having four sides. See *parallelogram, rectangle, square, trapezoid*.

Quadrivium (kwad-RIV-ee-um) **of Mathematics.** Plato's method of showing the relationship of all knowledge to mathematics, and one of the first classifications of mathematics. This was probably based on the Quadrivium of *Pythagoras*.

quantity. An amount, a number, or an expression that takes on a value.

quantum (plural, *quanta*). The smallest "package" of radiant energy.

quantum mechanics is a branch of physics concerned

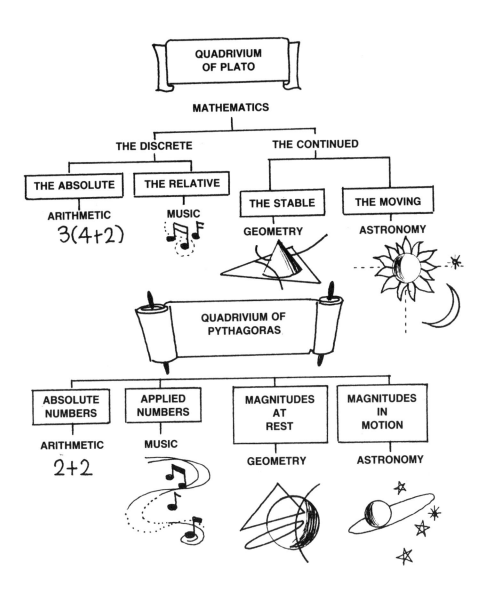

with group behavior. There is no way to predict, accurately, the individual behavior of *subatomic particles,* only the probabilities. See *Planck; Heisenberg.*

quark. In physics, a hypothetical particle, believed to be a basic unit of which *elementary practicles* are made. No one has ever seen a quark.

quart. A measure of capacity, such as 2 pints or 0.946 liters. See *tables, p. 244, 246.*

quarter. One of four equal parts into which something is divided. Also, the common term used in the United States and Canada for the coin worth ¼ of a dollar, or approximately 25 cents.

quartic equation. An *equation* of the fourth *degree.*

quartile. A set of *scores* can be divided into four equal parts. The *median* divides the scores into a lower and an upper half. The median is sometimes called the second quartile. The measure that divides the lower half into two equal parts is called the first quartile, and that which di-

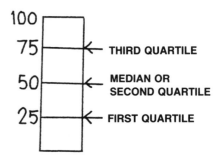

vides the upper half is the third quartile. The 25th, 50th, and 75th *percentiles* are the 1st, 2nd, and 3rd quartiles.

quaternions (kwa-TER-nee-onz). One of the basic laws of number systems is the *commutative property* of multiplication; for example, $6 \times 5 = 5 \times 6$. In the 1830s and 1840s, *Hamilton* freed algebra from centuries of tradition by setting up a system, quaternions, in which the commutative property of multiplications does not apply: $a \times b \neq b \times a$. He thus made possible many new algebras, just as freedom from thinking strictly in terms of *Euclidean geometry* made the *non-Euclidean geometries* possible. Quaternions were the first of many kinds of *hypercomplex numbers.*

Quetélet (kay-te-LAY), **Lambert Adolphe,** 1796–1874. A Belgian teacher of mathematics and science. He inspired and superintended the building of the royal observatory at Brussels and became its director. He planned a census in 1829. Collecting figures on the influence of sex, age, education, etc., on crimes, he was amazed at the accuracy of predictions that were possible. His studies of *statistics* and *probability* showed human traits could be predicted. This was the first time that conclusions about society were drawn from statistics.

quinary, (KWY-neh-ree) **system of numeration.** A numeration system using *base* five.

quindecagon. A *polygon* with fifteen sides.

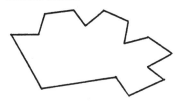

quintal. In the *metric system,* a unit of weight equal to 100 *kilograms.* See *table, p. 248.*

quintic equation. An equation of the fifth *degree.*

quintunx. An arrangement of five objects in a square or rectangle, one at each corner and one in the middle.

quire (KWYR). A set of twenty-four sheets of paper of equal size.

quotient. The name commonly given to the result when one number is divided by another. For example, 5 is the quotient resulting from the *division* of 10 by 2. In general, the term is used as follows:

$$9 \div 2 \quad \text{OR} \quad \frac{9}{2} \quad \text{OR} \quad 2\overline{)9}$$

MEANS

$$9 = \square \times 2 + \triangle$$

QUOTIENT   REMAINDER

Since $9 = 4 \times 2 + 1$, 4 is the quotient and 1 is the remainder.

R

R. The capital letter R is used to designate the set of *real numbers*.

r. The lowercase letter r is an abbreviation for *radius, rate.* It is also used as a *variable* in such *formulas* as the one for distance, $d = rt$.

radian measure. Sometimes called *circular measure.* The unit is a radian, or any angle that, if placed with its *vertex* at the center of a circle, intercepts an *arc* equal to the length of the *radius* of the circle. The intercepted arc is the same length as the radius. Radian measure is too large for practical measurements such as surveying but is very useful in trigonometry and advanced mathematics.

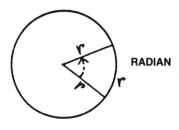

RADIAN

radical. An expression consisting of a phrase and a sign over it, called a radi<u>cal</u>. Expressions such as $\sqrt{36}$,

$\sqrt[3]{64}$, $\sqrt{5x^2}$, and so on are radicals. The symbol $\sqrt{}$ is called a radical sign.

radicand. The quantity under a *radical* sign.

radius of a circle. A *line segment* with one endpoint the center of a *circle*. The other endpoint is on the circle.

radius of a sphere. A *line segment* whose one endpoint is the center of the sphere and whose other endpoint is on the sphere.

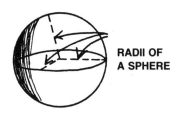

RADII OF A SPHERE

radix. Synonym for *base* (in a *notation system*). A base five system is called a system with a radix of five. Ten is the radix of our system of notation.

random sampling. Taking a *sample* from the population in which all members have the same chance of being included.

range. In *statistics,* the *absolute difference* between the greatest measure and the least measure in any set of *data.*

range of a relation or function. If a relation is a set of *ordered pairs*—(0, 1), (1, 2), (2, 3), (3, 4)—the range of the relation is the set of second members of the number pairs. In this case the set {1, 2, 3, 4} is the range of this relation or function. See *domain.*

rate of interest. Usually expressed in percent form; for example, 6% per year. See *table of formulas, p. 243.*

rate of speed. If a plane flies 1,200 miles in 2 hours, the ratio of the number 1,200 and 2 is usually called the rate and is expressed as 600 miles per hour.

ratio. The *quotient* of two numbers. It can be written $\frac{a}{b}$ or a:b where b ≠ 0. See *fractions.*

Also an *ordered pair* of numbers. To compare two sets, we might try to match *elements.* We can say the ratio between the sets is 12 to

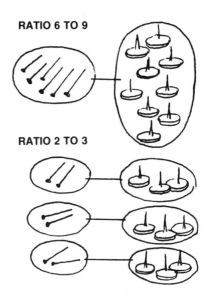

RATIO 6 TO 9

RATIO 2 TO 3

18, or 6 to 9, or 2 to 3. All name the same ratio.

rational expression. An expression stated as the *quotient* of two *polynomial* expressions over the *integers.* It is understood that the denominator cannot be zero.

$$\frac{3x+1}{x}, \frac{3y}{18}, \frac{x \times 3x+1}{x+1}, x+1$$

All of the above are rational expressions. See *rational number.*

rationalization. The *denominator* or *divisor* of a *rational expression*. The removal of the *radicals* in the denominator in an expression without changing the value. For example:

$$\frac{3}{\sqrt{5}} = \frac{3\sqrt{5}}{5}$$

rational number. A number that can be expressed in the form of a *fraction* as $\frac{a}{b}$ where a and b are any *integers* and $b \neq 0$. Sometimes rational numbers are defined in terms of ordered pairs of integers: (a, b) where $b \neq 0$. Equality of rational numbers means (a, b) = (c, d) if and only if ad = bc. Addition of rational numbers means:

(a, b) = (c, d) =
(ad + bc, bd).

The rational number (a, 1) or $\frac{a}{1}$ is written a.

$$\frac{1}{2}, \frac{3}{4}, \frac{10}{2}$$

rational number in arithmetic. A *fractional number*.

ray. A *point* in a *line* divides the line into two half-lines. A ray is a half-line, together with the point. The point is called the *endpoint* of the ray. A ray is shown as:

$$\overrightarrow{AB}$$

$\overrightarrow{AB}$ means "Ray AB" with endpoint A. $\overrightarrow{BA}$ means that the endpoint is B. See *arrow*.

real numbers. The set of real numbers consists of the union of the set of *rational numbers* and the set of *irrational numbers*.

real plane. A *coordinate* system on a plane in which an *ordered pair* of *real numbers* can be associated with every point on the plane.

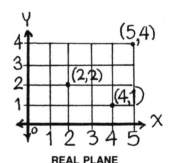

REAL PLANE

ream. A package of five hundred sheets of paper.

reasoning, mathematical. See *deductive reasoning; induction, mathematical*.

reciprocal. See *multiplicative inverse.*

$$\frac{2}{5} \quad \frac{5}{2}$$

rectangle. A *parallelogram* with one angle a *right angle.* This makes all the angles right angles.

rectangular numbers. Numbers that can be represented by dots or other symbols in the shape of a *rectangle.* The number 8 may be represented as ● ● ● ● or ● ●

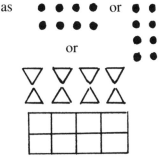

rectangular parallelepiped. A right *parallelepiped* with rectangular bases.

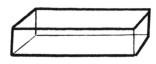

A RECTANGULAR
PARALLELEPIPED IS
ALSO A RECTANGULAR
RIGHT PRISM

rectangular right prism. A right *prism* whose faces are rectangular regions.

reducing fractions to lowest terms. A phrase used to mean the removal of the *greatest common factor* of the *numerator* and *denominator* of a fraction. When the largest common factor of the numerator and denominator is 1, the fraction has been reduced to its lowest terms, or simplest form.

$$\frac{8}{12} = \frac{2}{3}$$

redundant number. See *abundant number.*

referent. The object or idea to which a name refers. In 37, "3" refers to or represents 3 groups of 10. The referent is the 3 groups of 10 things.

reflection. Mirroring an image or counterpart; one of the *invariant* properties of Euclidean *geometry.*

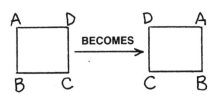

reflexive property of equality. For each number, a, a = a is a true statement. A quantity is equal to itself.

reflex angle. Any angle whose measure is more than 180° and less than 360°.

REFLEX ANGLE

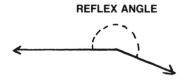

region of a plane. Part of a *plane*. The interior of a *simple closed curve* is a region. The picture shows a rectangular region bounded by a rectangle.

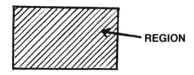

REGION

regrouping. Another name, used mostly in schools, for the *associative property for addition* and *for multiplication*.

$$3 + (4 + 6) = (3 + 4) + 6$$
$$3 \times (9 \times 4) = (3 \times 9) \times 4$$

regular polygon. A *polygon* in which all sides are the same length and all interior angles are the same measure.

REGULAR POLYGONS

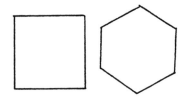

relation. A set of *ordered pairs*.

X	Y	
1	2	(1,2)
2	4	(2,4)
3	6	(3,6)
4	8	(4,8)

relationship, one-to-one. See *correspondence*.

relative error. Ratio of the *greatest possible error*, or *G.P.E.*, to the total measure. If the relative error is given as a percent, then it is called the percent of error.

$$\text{relative error} = \frac{\text{G.P.E.}}{\text{measure}}$$

relatively prime whole numbers. Numbers whose only common factor is 1. For example, 5 and 9 are relatively prime numbers.

remainder. In $9 \div 2$, which means $9 = \square \times 2 + \triangle$, $\triangle$ is the remainder. $9 \div 2$ is $9 = 4 \times 2 + 1$, so 1 is the remainder. $\triangle = 1$.

$$11 \div 4 \quad \text{MEANS}$$

$$11 = \underset{\uparrow}{\square} \times 4 + \underset{\uparrow}{\triangle}$$

PLACEHOLDER   **PLACEHOLDER**
FOR FACTOR   **FOR REMAINDER**

$$11 = \boxed{2} \times 4 + \boxed{3}$$

renaming numbers. A number has many names. $\frac{8}{10}$ may be renamed $\frac{4}{5}$. $5(2 + 3)$ may be renamed 25. 14 may be renamed $10 + 4$.

repeating decimal. A *decimal* in which one digit repeats itself endlessly or a group of digits repeat themselves endlessly:

$$.23333 \ldots$$
$$.257257 \ldots$$

Any repeating decimal can be expressed in the form $\frac{a}{b}$ when a and b are integers and $b \neq 0$. Therefore, a repeating decimal represents a rational number.

repetend. The name given to the *digit* or group of digits that repeat endlessly in the decimal form of a *rational number*. See *repeating decimal*.

replacement set. The *set* of numbers whose names are used as replacements for the *variable* in an *equation* or *inequality*.

result. The outcome of one or more *operations*, or the end in a proof.

resultant of two forces. One force that is equivalent to two forces. See *force, component of*.

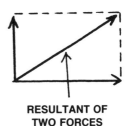

RESULTANT OF
TWO FORCES

revolution. Consider a *ray* with a fixed *endpoint*. If a ray moves about a fixed point in a *plane,* it will come back to its initial position. We say the ray has turned through one revolution.

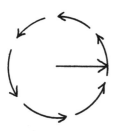

Rhind papyrus. A mathematical work of the ancient Egyptian scribe *Ahmes,* discovered in modern times by A. Henry Rhind. The main portion is now in the British Museum.

rhombus. A *parallelogram* with two adjacent sides equal in length. It can be shown that all four sides are the same length.

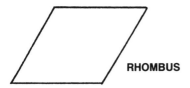

RHOMBUS

Riemann (REE-man), **Georg,** 1826–1866. A German mathematician and the founder of a *non-Euclidean geometry* which, like those of *Bolyai* and *Lobachevski,* was based on assuming a postulate different from *Euclid's fifth or parallel postulate.* He replaced the parallel postulate of Euclid with the postulate: Through a given point outside a given line there are no parallels to the given line. That is, any pair of lines must meet.

Riemann was also one of the founders of *topology.*

right. Direction on the *number line* to describe *greater than.* A number associated with a point to the right of a second point is greater than the number associated with the second point. −6 is greater than −10.

$$\xleftarrow{\quad\cdot\quad\cdot\quad\cdot\quad\cdot\quad\cdot\quad\cdot\quad}\rightarrow$$
−10 −9 −8 −7 −6 −5 −4

right angle. An angle of 90°.

right triangle. A triangle, one of whose angles is a right angle.

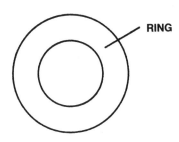

RING

ring. In geometry, the portion of a plane between two *concentric circles.* See *annulus.*

robot. A computer-controlled machine.

rod. A unit of measure. I acre contains 160 square rods. See *tables, p. 246.*

rods. See *Montessori rods, Napier's bones, Stern rods.*

Roman numerals. The notation system used by the Romans. The first ten numerals are I, II, III, IV, V, VI, VII, VIII, IX, and X. Other symbols are: L (50), C (100), D (500), and M (1,000).

root. A solution of an equation. 3 is a root of $2x = 6$ because $2 \times 3 = 6$. See *square root, cube root, quadratic formula.*

rotation. Turning around, as a wheel on its axis. One of the *invariant* properties.

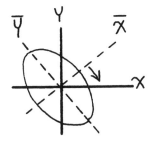

ROTATION OF
COORDINATE AXES

GEOMETRIC FIGURES ARE
ROTATED TO STUDY THEM
IN DIFFERENT POSITIONS

round angle. A rarely used term for an angle of 360°, sometimes called a perigon.

ROUND
ANGLE

rounded number. An approximate number. Usually a number expressed in some convenient unit so that its meaning in the situation can be more easily understood or used. 4,879,652 might be written as 5,000,000, rounded to the nearest million.

row. A line or arrangement running horizontally, as opposed to a *column,* which is a vertical arrangement.

```
1 2 3 4
2
3
4
```

rule. Sometimes a rule in mathematics is a procedure, as a rule for the order of operations. Sometimes it is a definition, as the rule of signs in multiplying integers. Sometimes a rule is a formula. The rule for finding the perimeter of a square is $p = 4s$.

rule or ruler. A *straightedge* with gradations or a *scale.*

rule of signs. See *Descartes.*

Russell, Sir Bertrand, 1872–1970. An English mathematician and philosopher. Early in the twentieth century he

published many important mathematical works, among them *Principia Mathematica* with *Whitehead.*

Rutherford, Ernest, 1871–1937. An English physicist who was the first to show that the *atom* had a *nucleus.* He also identified and named the *proton.* He studied radioactivity and atomic structure, but he never believed the nucleus would be a source of usable energy.

S

S. Abbreviation for *surface.*

s. Abbreviation for side. s represents the length of a side. It is used in such *formulas* as p = 3s.

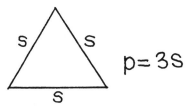

Saadia (SAH-di-a), **Gaon.** A tenth-century Egyptian-Babylonian-Jewish mathematician who mastered all the mathematics of his day and wrote on mathematics, time, infinity, proofs, uniqueness, medicine, astronomy, and music.

sample of a population. In *statistics,* a group of people selected at random from a population. Polls used in politics and TV program ratings use a sample group of people selected to represent a cross-section of a larger population to which they belong.

sample point. One of the possible outcomes of an *event,* named by an *ordered pair* of numbers. See *sample space.*

sample space. In *statistics,* all the possible outcomes of an experiment. Each outcome is called a *sample point.*

Sand Reckoner, The. One of *Archimedes*'s papers on arithmetic. In it he proves that no matter how large a number is—even a number representing all the grains of sand that would fill a sphere starting at the earth's center, with its circumference touching the sun—it is possible to represent this number as a *finite* number.

satisfy. To fulfill conditions.

satisfy an equation. A number such as 5 satisfies the equation 2x + 3 = 13, because when x is replaced by 5, 2(5) + 3 = 13 is a true *statement.* A number satisfies an equation if a true statement is formed when the *variable* is replaced by the numeral for the number.

scalar. A number written in front of a *matrix* to show the

$$2 \begin{pmatrix} 1 & 5 & 6 \\ 3 & 2 & 4 \end{pmatrix}$$

SCALAR

operation of multiplication to be performed on every element in the matrix by that number.

scale. A measuring device that is a set of units, usually equally spaced. Thermometers, rulers, and balances for weighing are all scales. See also *scale drawing.*

scale drawing. One which is in direct *proportion* to the subject drawn. It may be smaller, as a map, equal in size, or larger than the original object, as a billboard.

scalene triangle (SKAY-lean). A triangle with no two sides congruent.

SCALENE TRIANGLE

Schrödinger, Erwin, 1887–1961. A Viennese physicist who proposed that electrons were patterns of standing *waves.*

scientific notation. A way of writing numbers by expressing a number as a product of two *factors.* One factor is an integral *power* of ten, and the other is a factor between 1 and 10. For example, 2,950,000 can be written 2.95×10^6.

score. The equivalent of 20. "Four score and seven years ago" is $4 \times 20 + 7 = 87$.

In testing, a score is the performance of an individual or a group, shown by a numeral, letter, or other mark.

scruple. In *apothecaries' weight,* 20 grains. See *table, p. 244.*

secant of a circle. A line that intersects a circle at two points is called a secant.

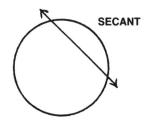

SECANT

second. A measure of time, 1/60 of a minute. A measure of distance on the earth's surface, part of a *degree* of distance. See *table, p. 247.*

An *ordinal number,* indicating a position in an *array.*

section, golden. See *golden section.*

sector of a circle. Part of a circular *region* bounded by two *radii* and the *intercepted arc.*

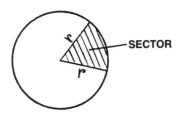

segment. See *line segment.* Segment of a circle refers to the region bounded by an *arc* of the circle and its *chord.*

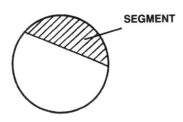

selling price. The price of an item to the buyer, usually the *cost* of the item plus the *overhead,* plus the *profit* the merchant intends to make.

semi. A prefix meaning *half.* A semicircle is one of the two half-arcs of a circle, determined by the endpoints of a *diameter.*

sentence, mathematical. A sentence that uses numerals, symbols, and sometimes words. It may be true or false. Two expressions with a symbol of numerical relationship between them. For example, the following are mathematical sentences:

$7 > 3$ (7 is greater than 3)
$4 + 2 = 6 + 0$
$7x + 3 = 17$
$x^2 + 3x + 2 = 0$

See *compound, conditional open sentence, connective.*

separation. The division of a *set* into two or more *subsets.*

$$SET\ A = \{1, 2, 3, 4, 5, 6\}$$
$$SET\ B = \{2, 4, 5, 6\}$$
$$SET\ C = \{1, 3\}$$
SUBSETS

septennial. Occurring every seven years.

septillion. In the United States and France, 1 followed by 24 zeros. In England and Germany, 1 followed by 42 zeros.

sequence, number. A sequence is a set of numbers associated with the *counting numbers*. The numbers must be in a certain order. For example, 1, 3, 5, 7, and 9 is a sequence of terms that can be associated with the positive integers 1, 2, 3, 4, and 5. There must be a rule for finding any term of the sequence. The sequence 1, 3, 5, 7, and 9 progresses by 2. Its general term is $2n - 1$.

An *arithmetic progression* and a *geometric progression* are both examples of number sequences. A sequence is sometimes defined as a *function* whose *domain* is the *positive integers*.

series. The indicated sum of the terms of a *sequence*. For example, 1, 3, 5, 7, and 9 are terms of a sequence. $1 + 3 + 5 + 7 + 9$ is a series.

set. An *undefined term* in mathematics. The term set is useful in talking about collections or groups of objects. The objects may be things, numbers, ideas, and so on. Each object in a set is called a *member* or *element* of the set.

Sets are described by listing names of members, called the roster $\{1, 2, 3, 4, 5\}$. *Braces* are used to enclose the names of the members of a set. Sometimes a set is described by a *condition;* for example, the set of all *natural numbers* less than 6. It is only when we have made it clear which objects belong to the set and which do not, that we have a *well-defined set.*

set-builder notation. See *such that.*

set roster. See *description of a set.*

set selector. Let the possible *replacements* for the *variable* x in the sentence $x + 2 = 5$ be the set $\{1, 2, 3, 4\}$:

If $x = 1$, $1 + 2 = 5$ (false)
If $x = 2$, $2 + 2 = 5$ (false)
If $x = 3$, $3 + 2 = 5$ (true)
If $x = 4$, $4 + 2 = 5$ (false)

Thus, the sentence $x + 2 = 5$ is called a set selector in that it sorts the set $\{1, 2, 3, 4\}$ into two sets, one set $\{1, 2, 4\}$ whose members make the sentence false, and the other set $\{3\}$ that makes the sentence true.

set theory. The branch of mathematics concerned with *sets,* the *operations* on sets, and the *properties* concerning those operations on sets. Set theory has many applications in logic, chance and probability, geometry, and the higher branches of mathematics.

sexagesimal (sex-a-JES-a-mal) **system of numeration.** A numeration system using 60 as a base. See *Babylonian notation system.*

sextillion. In the United States and France, 1 followed by 21 zeros. In England and Germany, 1 followed by 36 zeros.

shadow reckoning. A method, used by the early Egyptians, of measuring heights by the sun's shadow.

short ton. In *avoirdupois weight,* 2,000 pounds, a ton.

sides of an angle. The two *rays* that comprise the angle are called sides.

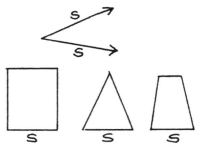

SIDES OF POLYGONS

sieve of Eratosthenes (e-ra-TOS-the-neez). A method worked out by *Eratosthenes* for finding all *prime numbers*

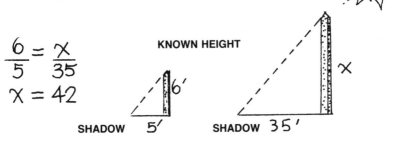

$$\frac{6}{5} = \frac{x}{35}$$

$$x = 42$$

KNOWN HEIGHT

6'

SHADOW 5'

SHADOW 35'

x

less than a particular number. Write the numbers from 2 to the particular number. After 2, cross out every second number. The first number left is a prime, 3, so cross out every third number. The next prime left is 5, so cross out every fifth number and continue.

2 3 4̸ 5 6̸ 7 8̸ 9̸
1̸0̸ 11 1̸2̸ 13 1̸4̸ 1̸5̸ 1̸6̸
17 1̸8̸ 19 2̸0̸ 2̸1̸ 2̸2̸
23 2̸4̸ 2̸5̸ 2̸6̸ 2̸7̸
2̸8̸ 29 3̸0̸

SIEVE OF ERATOSTHENES

signed numbers. Also called *directed numbers*. A term commonly used to describe the set of the negative numbers (numbers less than zero), zero, and the positive numbers (numbers greater than zero). A *number line* is usually used to picture the numbers.

significant digits. Those which are important in expressing the number of units used to find the measure of an object. The following *digits* are considered significant:

1. Each nonzero digit.

12

2. Each zero digit between nonzero digits.

102

3. Each zero digit that is not used only for the purpose of locating the decimal point.

102.0

similar figures. Two figures having the same shape, if not the same size.

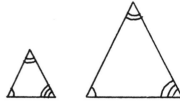

SIMILAR FIGURES

similarity correspondence. The *correspondence* between *vertices* of two *polygons* in which the corresponding angles are *congruent* and the corresponding sides are proportional in measure.

simple closed curve. A closed curve that does not cross itself.

SIMPLE CLOSED CURVES

simple closed figure. See *closed plane figure.*

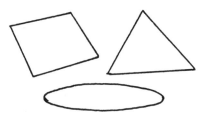

SIMPLE CLOSED FIGURES

simple condition. A requirement expressed by an *open sentence.* In the *condition* $x + 4 = 6$, the replacement for x is 2. It answers the requirement because $2 + 4 = 6$ is true.

simple event. A subject in an experiment of all possible happenings called an *event* space. When a penny is tossed it can land either head or tail up {H, T}. A simple event is {H} or {T}. Used in *probability.*

simple form of ratios. A *ratio* in which the two terms are *whole numbers* and the whole numbers have the number 1 as the *greatest common factor.*

$$3:7 \quad \frac{3}{7}$$

simple interest. See *interest.*

simple sentence. A mathematical statement with one thought. Some simple sentences are:

$$4 + 3 = 7$$
$$4 > 3$$
$$4 < 5$$

simplify. To write a shorter form of a *numeral* or *algebraic expression.* For example, to simplify $[2 (3 + 5) - 7]$, do all the operations called for until the expression has reached its simplest form, 9. 5x is $2x + 3x$ in simpler form.

simultaneous equations. Two *linear equations* with *variables* whose *graphs* intersect at one point. They are said to have a common *solu-*

tion. Some authors use "si-multaneous equations" to mean a system of equations that may or may not have a common solution.

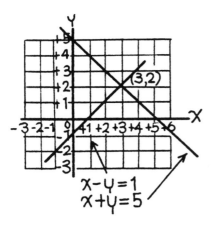

SIMULTANEOUS EQUATIONS

sine ratio of a right triangle. The *ratio* of the measure of the side opposite angle A to the measure of the *hypotenuse* is called the sine of the angle. The sine of ∠ A is usually abbreviated sin A. See *trigonometric function.*

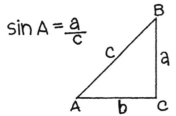

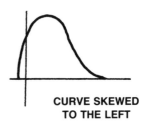

CURVE SKEWED TO THE LEFT

skewed curve. A curve that lacks *symmetry* with respect to a vertical line. In statistics, a curve not perfectly *bell-shaped,* but whose highest point is to the left of the *median* (negatively skewed) or to the right (positively skewed).

MEDIAN

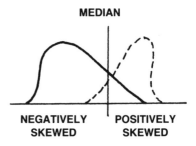

NEGATIVELY SKEWED   POSITIVELY SKEWED

skew lines. Two lines that do not lie in any one plane.

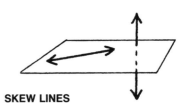

SKEW LINES

slant height of a right circular cone. The length of an element of a surface of the cone.

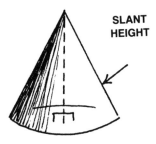

SLANT
HEIGHT

slide rule. An instrument for multiplying, dividing, extracting roots, and obtaining powers of numbers mechanically through the use of sliding logarithmic scales. The slide rule has almost entirely been replaced by calculators and computers.

slope. The rate at which a curve rises or falls per horizontal unit. The slope of a nonvertical line is expressed in terms of *coordinates* of any two points:

$$\text{slope} = \frac{(y_2 - y_1)}{(x_2 - x_1)}$$

small circle. See *circle, small; circle, great.*

smaller than. See *less than.*

software. A computer program; directions to a computer in mathematical form.

solid figure. See *space figure.* A solid refers to a space figure.

solid geometry. See *space geometry.*

solution. Any number from the *domain* (replacement set) of the *variable* that makes the *open sentence* a true statement. For example, from the set of numbers $\{1, 2, 3, 4, \ldots\}$, the number 4 is a solution of $3x + 2 = 14$ because $3 \times 4 + 2 = 14$.

solution set. The solution set or *truth set* of an *open sentence* is the set that contains all the solutions and only the solutions of the open sentence.

solve. To find the *solution set* to a *mathematical sentence* involving *variables.*

soroban. A Japanese *abacus.*

space. The *set* of all *points.* A three-dimensional *region.*

space curve. A curve in space, such as a *helix.* The

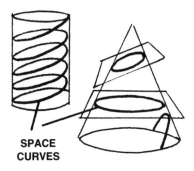

SPACE CURVES

intersection of two surfaces.

space figure. A set of points that may have one, two, or three dimensions. *Cubes, spheres,* and *pyramids* are space figures. Sometimes they are called solids, solid geometrical figures, or solid shapes.

SPACE FIGURES

space geometry. The study of three-dimensional space and *space figures.* Sometimes called solid geometry.

specific gravity. In a solid, the *ratio* of the weight per given *volume* to an equal volume of water.

$$\text{specific gravity} = \frac{\text{weight of given volume}}{\text{weight of same volume of water}}$$

speed. Distance traveled per unit of time. See *table of formulas, p. 243.*

speed of light. Light travels at approximately 186,000 miles per second. The symbol for the speed of light is c.

speed of sound. In dry air at 32°F or 0°C (the point at which water freezes), sound travels at approximately 760 miles per hour at sea level.

sphere. A *set of points* in *space* such that every point is equidistant from a point called the *center.* See *table of formulas, p. 242.*

spiral. A coil shape on a *plane* surface.

spread sheet. A computer ledger.

square. A *rectangle* having two adjacent sides of equal length. It can be shown that

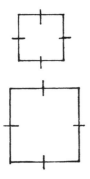

all four sides are the same length.

square numbers. 1, 4, 9, 16, etc. Numbers that can be represented by dots in the form of a square.

square of a number. A number raised to the second *power:* $5^2 = 25$. A number multiplied by itself: $5 \times 5 = 25$.

square root of a number. A number that, when raised to the second *power,* produces the given number. For example, a square root of 9 is $+$ or -3. The symbol for square root is $\sqrt{\ }$. The symbol calls for a " $+$ " value only. See *principal square root; table of square roots,* p. 252.

squaring the circle. See *circle, squaring the.*

stadium paradox of Zeno. One of his four *paradoxes,* in which he stated that a given interval of time or space can be equal to twice that same amount of time or space.

IF THREE ROWS OF PEOPLE ARE SITTING LIKE THIS:

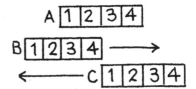

AND AT THE SAME INSTANT THE PEOPLE IN ROW B MOVE TO THE RIGHT, WHILE THOSE IN ROW C MOVE TO THE LEFT, UNTIL THEY ARE SEATED LIKE THIS:

A | 1 | 2 | 3 | 4 |
B | 1 | 2 | 3 | 4 |
C | 1 | 2 | 3 | 4 |

B HAS PASSED ALL FOUR OF C, BUT ONLY TWO OF A. THUS A GIVEN INTERVAL OF TIME OR SPACE IS EQUAL TO ITS DOUBLE.

standard. A basis for comparison.

**standard description of a
solution set.** A *solution set*
whose *elements* are not tabu-
lated or listed. The solution
set of the *condition* x > ⅔ can
be described only as {x|x > ⅔}:
read, "The set of all x's *such
that* each x is greater than
⅔."

standard deviation. See *deviation, standard.*

standard form. A form generally accepted as a way of
writing an *algebraic expression* so that the *exponents* of
one of the *variables* are in
descending order:

$$ax^4 + bx^3 + cx^2 + ax + e$$

**standard form of a quad-
ratic equation.** A *quadratic equation* in which the
term containing the *second
power* is written first: $8x^2 +$
⅔x + 6 = 0. The general form
$ax^2 + bx + c = 0$ where a, b,
and c are *real numbers* and
a ≠ 0.

**standard name of a nu-
meral.** In the base ten system,
for example, 347 is in standard form. It means 300 +
40 + 7. See *expanded notation.*

standard number of a set.
The *cardinal number* of *elements* in a *set.*

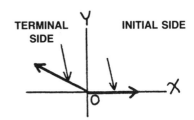

**standard position of an an-
gle.** In *trigonometry* an angle
is said to be in standard position if the *vertex* is the point
of the origin of the *x*- and
y-axes and the initial side of
the angle is on the positive
x-axis.

TERMINAL SIDE · INITIAL SIDE

standard units of measure.
Units of measure that are accepted by agreement. They
are uniform and unvarying.
See *tables, pp. 244–249.*

statement. A *mathematical
sentence* that is either true or
false, but not both.

statistics, descriptive. The
branch of mathematics that

collects and interprets information known as *data* and tabulates and analyzes it. See *bell-shaped curve.*

statute mile (also called land mile). A land measure, 5,280 feet in length. In many parts of the world the *kilometer* is used as the standard measure of land distance. See *tables, pp. 244, 245, 249.*

Stern blocks. A set of colored blocks named for educator Catherine Stern. They are graduated in size, each ¾″ larger than the previous one, and similar to the blocks developed by Countess *Montessori.*

Stevinus (ste-VEE-nus), **Simon,** 1584–1620. A Dutch mathematician known for his work in applied mathematics, particularly the triangle of *forces.* He used the idea of *exponents* to show the *power* to which a quantity is to be raised. His were among the first books devoted to the theory of *decimals.* His symbolism was quite awkward compared with today's. For example, 6.879 would be written: 6 ⓪8 ① 7 ② 9 ③.

stone. In English measure, the equivalent of 14 pounds.

straight angle. An angle whose measure is 180°.

STRAIGHT ANGLE

straightedge. An instrument used for making straight lines in geometric drawings. Unlike a *ruler* it has no measuring scale.

straight line. See *line.*

string theory. Elementary particles can be thought of as vibrating strings instead of points, as in the *quantum theory*, Superstring theory makes it possible to join all four fundamental *forces* as different aspects of a single principle. In superstring theory there are nine dimensions in space + time, making ten dimensions.

strong force. The *force* that keeps atomic nuclei together. It is one of the four known forces in physics.

structure of a system. There are different mathematical

systems. Each has its own structure. A number system has a *set* of *elements* (numbers); it may have two operations ($+$ and $\times$) and certain properties of the operations, such as the *commutative property*.

suan pan (SWAN-PAN). A Chinese *abacus*.

subatomic particles. Particles smaller than atoms.

subscript. A numeral, letter, or word written to the right and just below another numeral. It may be used to indicate the *base* of the *notation system* of the numeral. The numeral 432_{FIVE} indicates the name of the number in *base five*. Subscripts are also used to distinguish *points* and *coordinates,* and to distinguish terms, such as a_1, a_2, a_3, and so on.

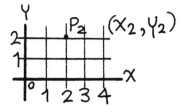

subset. If every *element* of *set* A is also a member of set B, then set A is a subset of set B and we say that set A is included in set B. For example, if set A consists of the letters a, b, and c, and set B consists of the letters a, b, c, and d, then set A is a subset of set B. See *proper subset*.

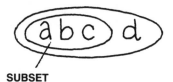

SUBSET

substitution in algebra. The usual reference is to the *replacement* of a *variable* by a numeral.

substitution in codes. See *codes*.

subtend in geometry. To be opposite to, as a chord subtends the arc it cuts on a circle.

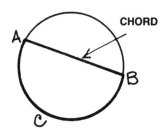

SUBTENDED ARC, $\overset{\frown}{ACB}$

subtraction. Subtraction is the *inverse* of *addition*. For example, $7 - 4$ is a number, n, so that $n + 4 = 7$. Since $3 + 4 = 7$, then $7 - 4 = 3$.

$$\square + 3 = 7$$
$$\boxed{4} + 3 = 7$$
$$7 - 3 = 4$$

In general, if a and b are two whole numbers, and a is greater than or equal to b, $a - b$ is a number, c, such that $c + b = a$. $a - b = c$ means $c + b = a$. See *subtrahend, minuend, operation*.

subtrahend. The number or *term* to be subtracted.

$$7 - 3$$

succession. *Numerals, terms,* or *operations* that follow each other in a definite order.

successor. Any *term* that immediately follows any other term in a *sequence*. In 1, 2, 3, 4, 5 . . . the successor of 1 is 2, the successor of 2 is 3, and so on.

such that. Usually referred to in *set-builder notation*. The symbol for "such that" is |

or :. $\{x \mid x + 5 = 7\}$ is read: The set of all x's such that $x + 5 = 7$. The symbol $\{\mid\}$ is called a set builder.

sum. In addition, the result of adding two or more numbers or *addends*.

sum property of "less than." For all real numbers a, b, and c, if $a < b$ then $a + c < b + c$. Often called *addition property of inequalities*.

sunya. The Hindu word for zero. Arabian mathematicians translated it as "sifr," meaning empty, which became "cipher." Later, it became the Latin word "zephirum," which eventually became zero.

supercomputer. See *computer*.

superconductivity. The ability of a conductor to carry electric current without any resistance. This allows current to flow with no loss of energy. The principle was first discovered by a Dutch physicist, H. K. Onnes, in 1911.

superconductor. A material that can carry current with no loss of energy. At first the material depended on extreme cold—near absolute zero ($-273.2°$C.). In 1987 a ceramic was invented that became a superconductor at $-238°$. The search is for a superconductor at normal temperatures.

superstring theory. See *string theory*.

supplementary angles. Two angles the sum of whose measure is 180°. Each is the supplement of the other.

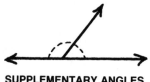

SUPPLEMENTARY ANGLES

surd. Sometimes used for an *irrational number*. $\sqrt{7}$, $\sqrt[3]{12}$, and $\sqrt{½}$ are examples of surds. The *radicands* are *rational*.

surface. A surface consists of *sets* of *points*. Usually, surface is *undefined* in geometry. There are plane surfaces such that a straight line joining any two of its points lies completely in the plane. There are curved surfaces of which no

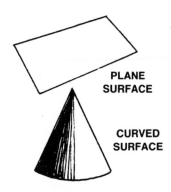

PLANE SURFACE

CURVED SURFACE

part is a plane. A surface may consist of plane and curved surfaces.

syllogism (SIL-oh-JIZ-um). In logic, an argument, usually with three parts:
1. A major premise or general statement.
2. A minor premise or specific statement.
3. A conclusion based on the above two.
For example:
1. All persons living in New York City live in New York State (major premise).
2. Henry lives in New York City (minor premise).
3. Henry lives in New York State (conclusion).

Sylvester, James, 1814–1897. An English mathematician and professor. Although his best-known contributions are in higher algebra, he wrote valuable papers on the theory of numbers and prime numbers. While at Johns Hopkins University, where he was the first professor of mathematics, he founded the *American Journal of Mathematics* in 1878.

symbol. A letter, numeral, or mark that represents a number, operation, or relation. See *table of symbols, pp. 237–240.*

1, 2, 3, □, x, +

symmetric. A relationship with the property that if a is related to b, then b is related in the same manner to a. If a = b then b = a. This statement demonstrates the symmetry property of equality.

symmetry in geometry. The *correspondence* of parts of a figure on opposite sides of a point, line, or plane. The *isosceles triangle* is symmetric with respect to the line through vertex B, perpendicular to the base AC.

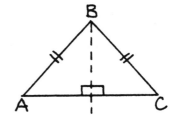

synthesis. The combination of elements into a whole. *Analysis* and synthesis are two methods used in mathematical thinking.

T

t. t-score in statistics is a standardized score. The *mean* is 50 and the *standard deviation* is 10.

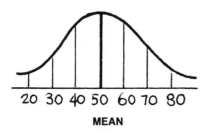

MEAN

Abbreviation for *temperature, ton, time*.

When used in a *formula* such as d=rt, t is a *variable* that stands for a numeral.

table. An arrangement of numerals, letters, or signs, usually in *rows* and *columns,* to show facts or relationships between them in a compact form. For example, the cost of 1 to 4 gallons of gasoline at $1.25 a gallon may be shown in a table:

NUMBER OF GALLONS	1	2	3	4
COST	1.25	2.50	3.75	4.50

tangent of an acute angle. In a right triangle, the *ratio* of the measure of the side opposite an acute angle to the measure of the side *adjacent* to the same acute angle.

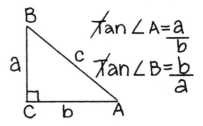

tangent to a circle. A *line* in the *plane* of a *circle* that intersects the circle in one and only one *point*.

tangram. A puzzle made by Chinese mathematicians about 4,000 years ago that showed how shapes are related. It was basically a square made of

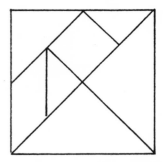

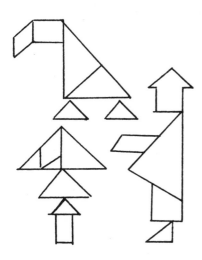

seven pieces. Hundreds of pictures can be made with these seven pieces.

target population. In *statistics,* the set of numbers, people, etc., about which information is desired.

Tartaglia (tar-TAL-ya), **Niccolo,** 1499–1557. An Italian mathematician whose solution for *cubic equations* is often credited unjustly to *Cardano.* His work on arithmetic and numbers gives an excellent account of methods in use at the time and is one of our chief sources of information. He also described the business customs of the day

and a number of mathematical puzzles for amusement, some of which go back to Hindu and Arabic mathematicians. Many of his puzzles were included in later books.

temperature. The amount of heat in a body or in the air, as measured by a thermometer. The two standard units are the *Fahrenheit* scale and the *Celsius* scale.

ten. A number. The Latin word for ten is *decem.* See *decimal system, base ten.*

terminal point. To describe a movement from point A to point B, we may use a *directed line segment* or *vector.* Point A is called the initial point and point B the terminal point of the line segment.

terminal side of an angle. See *standard position of an angle.*

terminating. Coming to an end. See *decimal, terminating.*

term of an expression. A numerical expression is a numeral, or numerals joined with symbols of operation:

$$7, \frac{(8+2)}{3}, 6\times 7.$$

Algebraic expressions include numerical expressions and expressions formed with variables:

$$x, 3y, n^2, \frac{x+7}{9}.$$

Each part of an expression written as a sum is called a term. In

$$(x-y)+\frac{(x-y^2)}{x}-7,$$

the terms are:

$$x-y, \frac{(x-y^2)}{x}, \text{ and } -7.$$

In the *polynomial* $3n^2 + 6n - 9$, the terms are:

$$3n^2, 6n, \text{ and } -9.$$

terms of a fraction. The *numerator* and *denominator* of a fraction.

$$\frac{2}{3}$$

terms of a proportion. Any one of the *means* or *extremes*.

$\frac{3}{4} = \frac{6}{8}$. The terms are 3, 4, 6, and 8. See *proportion*.

$$3:4=6:8$$

terms of a sequence. The *members* of the *range* of a *sequence*.

$$1,3,5,7,9$$

ternary (TURN-eh-ree). Having to do with 3; having three *variables*. The ternary system of notation is *base* three.

tetrahedron (tet-ra-HEE-dron). A *polyhedron* of four faces. A *regular* tetrahedron is a pyramid whose base and faces are *congruent equilateral* triangles.

TETRAHEDRON

Thales (THAY-lees), 640–546 B.C. The founder of the first Greek school of mathematics

and philosophy. He was the teacher of *Pythagoras* and probably the first person to insist on *proof* in geometry. He is the first man known to have shown that the base angles of an *isosceles* triangle are *congruent* and vertical angles are congruent.

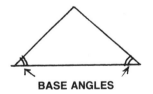

BASE ANGLES

VERTICAL ANGLES

theorem. A *proposition* to be proved. Theorems that have been proved true are used in proofs to prove other theorems true or false.

thermometer. An instrument used to measure *temperature*.

Thompson, Joseph John, 1856–1940. An English physicist and discoverer of the *electron* in 1897.

times. A word commonly used to indicate multiplication. 3×4 is read "three 4's" or "three times four." It also means $4 + 4 + 4$. The symbols for times are $\times$ and $\cdot$. With *variables,* no multiplication sign is needed, as in $3x$, abc, and $14x^2$. Parentheses can also indicate multiplication $x(a + b)$.

tolerance. The allowable error in a given measurement. If a part has a given measure of $5.125''$, the error allowable when making the part may be $.005''$ more than or less than the actual measure of $5.125''$. The standard way of writing the tolerance allowed is $5.125'' \pm .005''$, which means that any measure between $5.120''$ and $5.130''$ is acceptable.

ton. A measure of weight equal to 2,000 pounds, sometimes called a short ton. A *long ton* is 2,240 pounds. A register ton is a unit of ship capacity, not weight. It is 100 cubic feet. See *metric ton.*

A cargo ton is a unit of volume used for freight. It is 40 cubic feet. A kip is a half-ton or 1,000 pounds.

topology. Scientifically called *analysis situs;* popularly called rubber-sheet geometry. One of the more recent branches of mathematics, it deals with place and position, not quantity or measure. It concerns those properties of figures, like insides, outsides, and direction, which do not change no matter how the figures are bent, stretched, or distorted. In topology, these two figures are the same in the sense that they each have one inside and one outside:

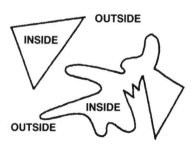

A DOUGHNUT HAS ONE INSIDE AND TWO OUTSIDES

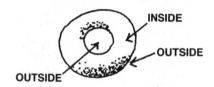

THE ORDER OF POINTS A, B, C, D ON THESE FIGURES HAS NOT CHANGED

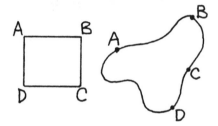

See *Klein bottle, Möbius strip, Brouwer's problem, torus, Euler, Riemann.*

torus (TOH-rus). A doughnut-shaped three-dimensional figure used in *topology.* Ordinarily we think of the hole as inside the doughnut, but in topology the hole is considered to be outside.

trajectory. The curve or path of a projectile, such as a bullet, as it goes through the air; also, the *curve* or *surface* that cuts all the curves or surfaces of a given *plane* or *space* at a constant angle.

transcendental number. An *irrational number* but not an *algebraic* one. Examples of transcendental numbers are π (3.1415926 . . .) and e, the symbol for the base of natural *logarithms* (2.7182818 . . .). *Cantor* proved that the number of transcendental numbers cannot be counted.

transform. To change the form of an *expression*. The word can also be used to refer to the expression or term that has been changed. For example, when ½ is changed to 50%, 50% can be called the transform.

transformation geometry. Description of a property that is not altered by certain change. *Klein* classified geometries according to their invariant properties of their figures. The four invariant properties of *Euclidean geometry* are *translation, rotation, reflection,* and *dilation.* In *topology,* figures are preserved although they are constantly deformed. See *affine geometry, point-set theory.*

transforming formulas. Solving *literal equations* for any *variable.* For example, in

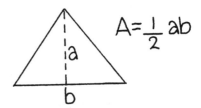

the formula for finding the area of a triangle, $A = \frac{1}{2}ab$ where A is the area, a is the measure of the altitude of the triangle, and b is the measure of the base of the triangle. If a is to be found, the tranformation of

$$A = \frac{1}{2}ab \text{ becomes } a = \frac{A}{(\frac{1}{2}b)}.$$

transitive property of congruence. In geometric figures:

If △ ABC ≅ △ DEF and
△ DEF ≅ △ GHJ, then
△ ABC ≅ △ GHJ.

This is true of all geometric figures.

transitive property of equality.

If $a = b$ and
$b = c$, then
$a = c$.

See *equality.*

translation. An exact duplication of a geometric figure.

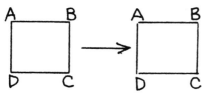

TRANSLATION OF ABCD

TRANSLATION OF COORDINATE AXES

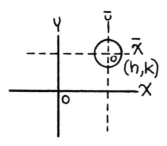

One of the *invariant* properties of *Euclidean geometry*.

transposition in codes. One of the principal ways of making a code by changing the position of the letters.

MEET ME TONIGHT

M	E	E	T		M	E
T	O	N	I	G	H	T

MTEOENTIGMHET

transversal. A straight *line* intersecting two or more lines at one point on each line. Line AB is the transversal.

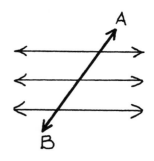

trapezium. A *quadrilateral,* no two of whose sides are *parallel.*

TRAPEZIUM

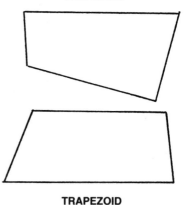

TRAPEZOID

trapezoid. A *quadrilateral*

with two, and only two, opposite sides *parallel*.

trapezoidal prism. A right *prism* whose bases are trapezoids.

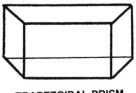

TRAPEZOIDAL PRISM

triangle. A *closed plane figure* with three sides. Triangles are classified by the relationship of the sides (see *equilateral, isosceles, scalene*) or by the measure of the angles (see *acute, obtuse, right angles*). See also *table of formulas, p. 241*.

triangular numbers. Numbers that can be represented by dots in the form of a triangle. The first three triangular numbers are 3, 6, and 10.

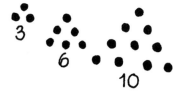

triangular pyramid. A pyramid that has a triangle as its base.

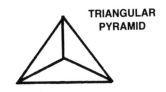

TRIANGULAR PYRAMID

triangular right prism. A right *prism* whose bases are triangles.

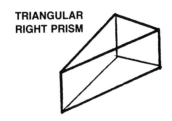

TRIANGULAR RIGHT PRISM

trichotomy property of real numbers. States that for any two *real numbers*, a and b, only one of the following is true:

     1. $a = b$
     2. $a < b$
     3. $a > b$

trigonometric function. If ϕ is one of the acute angles in a right-angle triangle, x is the side of the triangle nearest to ∅, y the side opposite the angle, and r the hypotenuse, the trigonometric functions are:

$\sin ∅ = y/r$; $\cos ∅ = x/r$; $\tan ∅ = y/x$; $\cos ∅ = 1/\sin ∅$; $\sec ∅ = 1/\cos ∅$; $\cot ∅ = 1/\tan ∅$.

The names of these functions are: *sine, cosine, tangent, cosecant, secant,* and *cotangent.*

trigonometry. The branch of mathematics that deals with the sides and angles of triangles and their measurements and relations. It also includes the study of *trigonometric functions* and their properties. See *Hipparchus.*

trihedral angle. A *polyhedral* angle with three faces.

**TRIHEDRAL
ANGLE**

trillion. A hundred billion, represented by 1 followed by 12 zeros in the United States and France, and 1 followed by 18 zeros in England and Germany.

trinomial. A *polynomial* of three terms. For example:

$$x^2 - 3x + 7.$$

trisection of the angle. Division of an angle into three equal parts. One of three classic problems of ancient Greek mathematics that cannot be solved using *Euclidean tools.* Attempting to find a solution, the Greeks discovered new mathematical concepts. See *cube problem; circle, squaring the.*

trivial. Of little importance. For any *natural number,* the trivial *divisors* are 1 and the number itself. The trivial divisors of 12 are 1 and 12.

Troy system of weights. A system for measuring precious metals. See *table, p. 244.*

true length. The actual length of an object. Because all measurement is approximate, there is always a difference between the true length and the *measured length.*

truth element. In a mathematical sentence containing a *variable,* one of the *elements* of the *replacement set* that makes the sentence true; the solution or one of the solutions. In

$$x + 2 = 5,$$
$$3 + 2 = 5 \text{ is true,}$$

so 3 is a truth element for the variable x.

truth set. A *set* whose *elements* are the solutions for a mathematical *sentence;* often called *solution set.* See *set selector.*

truth value. In *logic* each given statement has a truth value. The truth value may be true or false. The truth value of $3 + 4 = 8$ is false. The truth value of ''The surface of the earth is curved'' is true.

twelve-base for numeration. See *duodecimal system.*

twice. Two times, or double, as twice the quantity.

twin primes. Two *prime numbers* with a difference of 2. 3 and 5, 11 and 13, and 17 and 19 are examples of twin primes. So are 4967 and 4969. There are many twin primes.

two, system of numeration. See *binary system.*

U

U. The *universal set* is often denoted by U.

Uccello (oo-CHEL-oh), **Paolo,** 1397–1475. An Italian artist, who first used perspective. He was the first to make drawings on a *plane* surface, like paper or canvas, which gave the impression of having depth, or a third *dimension*.

uncertainty principle. See *Heisenberg*.

undefined terms. We define a new *term* by means of simpler terms, which are defined by still simpler terms. We finally reach terms that cannot be defined in a simpler way. Our definitions rest upon these undefined terms. Some undefined terms in geometry are *point* and *line*.

unequal. Not equal. The symbol is ≠. In 4 + 6 ≠ 11, we have the statement that 4 plus 6 is not equal to 11. In set A ≠ set B, we mean that the sets do not have exactly the same elements. See *inequality, equivalent*.

unification. The establishment of a relationship between elements that seem very different.

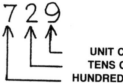

UNIT COLUMN
TENS COLUMN
HUNDREDS COLUMN

unit. "One" is a unit. The unit *column* in our *Hindu-Arabic notation system* refers to the first column to the left of the decimal point. In 729, the unit *digit* is 9.

union. The joining or combining of two or more things. The union of two *sets* A and B is the set of elements that belongs to A, to B, or to both A and B. For example, if set A = {1, 2, 3, 4} and set B = {3, 4, 5, 6}, then the union of the two sets is the set {1, 2, 3, 4, 5, 6}. The union of set A and set B is usually written A ∪ B (read: A union B or A cup B). The union can be used to define the sum of two numbers. Let

$$K = \{a, b, c\} \text{ and}$$
$$L = \{d, e, f, g\}, \text{ then}$$
$$\{a, b, c\} \cup \{d, e, f, g\} =$$
$$\{a, b, c, d, e, f, g\}$$

The number associated with set K is 3, with set L is 4, and with K ∪ L is 7. The sum of two numbers that are associated with two *disjoint sets* is the number associated with their union. See *addition, cup, join*.

unique. One and only one. The sum of two numbers is unique.

$$5+4=9$$

There is one and only one sum of two numbers. If a number is said to *correspond* to a unique point on a line, it means that the number corresponds to one and only one point. Two distinct points determine a unique line.

unique factorization theorem. Every *positive integer* can be expressed as the product of *prime factors* in one and only one way, regardless of the order of the factors.

$$3 \times 2 \times 2 = 12$$
$$2 \times 3 \times 2 = 12$$
$$2 \times 2 \times 3 = 12$$

uniqueness. If an operation is performed on any two elements of a set and the result is one and only one element, the operation has the property of uniqueness. For example, the sum of $7 + 8$ is the *unique* number 15. There is one and

only one number that is the sum of any two *real numbers*. The operations of addition and multiplication have this *property* in the set of real numbers.

unit angle. An angle of some measure that by common agreement will be the standard unit of angular measurement by which to measure all other angles.

unit circle. Circle whose center is at origin and whose radius is one unit.

unite. To join or combine so as to form a whole.

unit fraction. A fraction whose *numerator* is one and whose *denominator* is an *integer*. For example, ½, ⅕.

unit of measurement. A standard used, such as a pound, an inch, a gram, etc. Sometimes the word ''unit'' is used with a numeral, as:

6 units of work,
3 units of length.

units, fundamental. The units of length, mass, and time that form the basis for a system of measurement. For example: the *centimeter,* the *gram,* and the *second* are the fundamental units of the *cgs,* or *metric, system.*

unity element. Another name for the *identity element.*

universal set. The *set* from which all the subsets are selected in a discussion. For example, the *whole numbers* from 1 to 100 may be the universal set of our discussion. We may then discuss even numbers less than 100 and odd numbers less than 100, or some other subset. The universal set is often designated set U.

universe. The *set* of all *re-*

placements for a *variable* in a mathematical *condition.* See *universal set.*

unknown or unknown quantity. A symbol or a *placeholder* in a mathematical sentence. The unknown holds a place for the name of any element in the *replacement set.* The unknown is more commonly called a *variable.* In $5x + 3 = 13$, x is the unknown, or variable.

$$\Box, \triangle, x, y$$

unlike fractions. Fractions with different *denominators:*

$$\tfrac{2}{3}, \tfrac{2}{5}.$$

V

V. The Roman numeral for five. Abbreviation for *volume*.

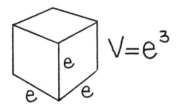

$$V = e^3$$

v. A *variable* used in *formulas* involving *velocity*, *volt*.

valid. Reasonable for a set of *assumptions*.

value. The value of a variable is any number in the *domain* of the variable. It is also the number named by an *expression* formed from numerals and signs of operations. The value of the expression $3(5 + 2)$ is 21. 21 is the standard name for $3(5 + 2)$. If an expression includes a *variable*, the value is the number named by the expression when the variable is replaced by a numeral. The value of $3x^2 + 7x$, when x is 2, is 26. See *place value*, *absolute value*.

vanishing point. In a perspective drawing, the place where parallel lines seem to come together.

variable. A letter or other *placeholder* in a mathematical expression. It may represent any *element* in a given *set* of elements. The set of elements is called the *domain* of the variable. Sometimes a variable is called an *unknown*. In $x^2 + 3x + 2 = 0$, x is the variable.

variable sentence (often called an open sentence). A mathematical sentence that contains at least one *variable*. It cannot be judged true or false until its variable is replaced by a numeral. $x + 5 = 7$ is a variable sentence. If x is replaced by 2, it is a true sentence. 2 is called a solution of $x + 5 = 7$.

variance. In *statistics*, the number that shows the amount of spread in a set of *scores*.

variation. See *direct variation, inverse variation.*

vector. In the drawing, there has been a movement, or displacement, from point A to point B. The displacement can be described as:

1. A *magnitude* of 100′.
2. A direction, parallel to the shore. To show the displacement geometrically, we use the *directed line segment* AB or vector AB. Point A is called the *initial point* and point B the *terminal point*. If from point B the boat moves to C, it seems logical that the vectors $\overrightarrow{AB}$ followed by $\overrightarrow{BC}$ are the same as a move directly from A to C. This is

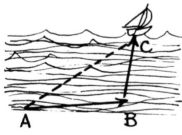

an example of "addition" of vectors. We say $\overrightarrow{AB} + \overrightarrow{BC} =$ AC. AC is called the vector resultant and can replace $\overrightarrow{AB}$ and $\overrightarrow{BC}$ as forces. So from a geometric representation, an algebra of vectors develops.

When the algebraic properties of vectors are abstracted from the geometry in which they originate, we enter vector space. See *force, components of.*

vector quantity. A quantity that has both *magnitude* and direction. See *vector.*

vectors, parallelogram of. If two vectors $\overrightarrow{AB}$ and $\overrightarrow{AC}$ are represented as two sides of a *parallelogram,* the other two sides can be drawn. The diagonal of the parallelogram is the vector *resultant* $\overrightarrow{AD}$. See *vector, force.*

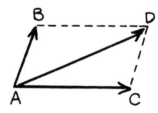

PARALLELOGRAM OF VECTORS

velocity. The unit of distance traveled, in a specified direction, per unit of time. See *table of formulas, p. 243.*

Venn, John, 1834–1923. An English mathematician who worked in *statistics, probability,* and *logic,* and whose name is given to *Venn diagrams.*

Venn diagrams. Diagrams to picture *sets* and the relationships between sets. The sets are represented by circles and their interiors, or by any shapes.

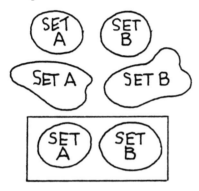

Sometimes the shapes are placed within a rectangle.

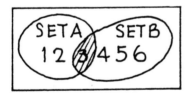

If set A = {1, 2, 3} and set B = {3, 4, 5, 6} their *intersection,* as shown in the diagram, is 3. Other relationships can easily be shown by Venn diagrams. See *subset, union, complementary set.*

vertex of an angle. The point of intersection of the two *rays* that form the angle.

vertex of a polygon. The point of intersection of any two adjacent sides of the polygon.

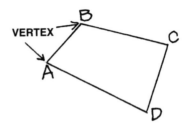

vertical. A vertical line is perpendicular to a horizontal line in the same plane.

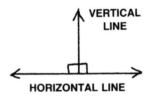

vertical angles. Nonadjacent angles formed by two intersecting lines. Angles 1, 3, and 2, 4 are vertical angles.

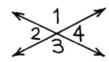

vertical form. An arrangement to facilitate computations. The vertical form of $80 + 6 + 23$ is

$$80$$
$$6$$
$$\underline{23}$$

vertices (VER-tih-sees). In *topology*, the points where the lines in a *network* cross. A, B, C, D, and E are vertices. See *vertex of a polygon*.

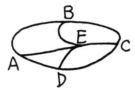

Vieta (vy-AY-ta), **François,** 1540–1603. A wealthy French lawyer and official whose hobby was mathematics. His many contributions included the use of letters as symbols for known and unknown quantities in algebra. He was the first to show that the value of π could be found from a formula instead of a complicated geometric figure. He wrote on equations and infinite converging series and did research in *analysis* and *trig-*

onometry. The Spanish accused him of sorcery because during a war between France and Spain he deciphered the Spanish code, which contained hundreds of symbols.

vinculum. A bar written over two or more quantities to show grouping. $\overline{8+4} \div 3$ means that the addition of 8 and 4 should be performed first. See *brackets, braces, parentheses*.

volt. A practical standard unit for measuring electrical force. 1 volt is needed to drive 1 *ampere* through 1 *ohm*.

volume. The number of *cubic* units in a solid. The volume of this rectangular solid is 24 cubic units.

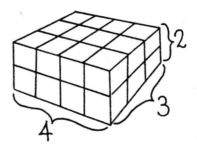

In sound, the loudness measured in *decibels*. See *table of formulas, p. 240*.

von Neumann, John, 1903–1957. One of the outstanding mathematicians of this century. Born in Hungary, he came to the United States in 1930 to teach mathematical physics at Princeton University. At twenty-eight he wrote a book on the *quantum* theory, which was one step in developing atomic energy. He built one of the first electronic *computers,* designed many nuclear devices, and contributed much to *game theory.* He said that even a skilled mathematician might know only 10% of the subject.

W

w. The abbreviation for *watt, width, weight.* It is used as a *variable* in such *formulas* as A = lw.

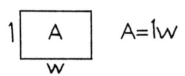

Wallis, John, 1616–1703. English mathematician, physician, clergyman, and philosopher. His publications on *conic sections* clarified the work of *Descartes.* He introduced the first systematic use of formulas in his writing on algebra. His most important work was the *Arithmetic of Infinities,* in which he extended the methods of Descartes and *Cavalieri.*

watt. A standard unit for measuring electrical power, equal to 1 *joule* per second.

wave. A point-to-point disturbance in a medium or in space. The points themselves do not move; the disturbance moves through them.

wave frequency. The number of waves that form and move out in a unit of time. It is measured in *hertz.*

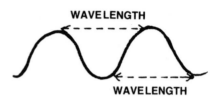

WAVELENGTH

wavelength. The length of the wave from crest to crest (or trough to trough).

weak force. One of the four known forces in physics, and the least understood.

week. A period of time; seven days. A workweek is the number of working days in a week.

Weierstrass (VY-er-straws), **Karl,** 1815–1897. One of the greatest German mathematicians of the nineteenth century, a teacher of *Kowalewski* and *Cantor.* He worked in mathematical *analysis,* in the theory of *functions,* and on ideas that had troubled mathematicians since ancient times, such as *infinity* and *irrational numbers.* His work eventually influenced the production of atomic energy and our present ideas of *infinite series.*

weight. Equals *mass* times *gravity.* For common measures of weight, see *tables, pp. 244, 248–249.*

well-defined set. A *set* described so that it is clear whether any *element* is or is not a member of the given set. "The set of all funny books," and "the set of all helpful boys" are not well defined because there can be differences of opinion about what or who should be included. "The set of all books on this table," and "the set of all girls over 6 feet tall in this school" are well defined.

Whitehead, Alfred North, 1861–1947. An English philosopher and mathematician who taught at the universities of London and Harvard. He used mathematical analysis in philosophy and in 1910 wrote his major work, *Principia Mathematica,* with *Bertrand Russell.* In it, the very structure of mathematics was probed. It is considered one of the greatest contributions to logic since *Aristotle.*

whole numbers. The set of numbers $\{0, 1, 2, 3, 4 . . .\}$ *Natural numbers,* or *counting numbers,* are usually not considered to include zero.

width. Measure from side to side.

word length. The number of *bits* usually processed by a computer as a single unit.

X,Y,Z

X. The Roman numeral for ten.

x. A symbol. A *variable,* or an *unknown* quantity.

$$2x = 10$$

x-axis. To locate any *point* in a *plane* by means of a pair of numbers, we select two intersecting lines in the plane as *axes.* The horizontal axis is called the x-axis. See *abscissa.*

x-intercept. A line intercepting the *x-axis.*

y. A symbol. A *variable* or an *unknown* quantity.

$$x^2 + y^2 = 16$$

y-axis. On a *coordinate plane,* the vertical *axis.* See *x-axis, coordinates.*

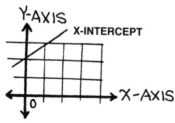

y-intercept. A line intercepting the *y-axis.*

yard. A unit of *linear measurement* equal to 36 inches. See *tables, pp. 244, 249.*

year. The period of time it takes the earth to make one complete orbit of the sun, approximately 365 days, 5 hours, 48+ minutes. The extra hours, minutes, and seconds are lumped into an extra day every four years, creating a "leap year."

z. A symbol. A *variable* or an *unknown* quantity.

zenith. The point of the celestial sphere directly above the observer.

Zeno (ZEE-know), 495–435 B.C. A Greek mathematician and philosopher, best known for his *paradoxes,* all of which deal with the idea of *infinity* of time and motion. It took mathematicians over two thousand years to solve them. Of the eight paradoxes he originated, four are known: The dichotomy, *Achilles and the tortoise, the arrow in motion,* and the *Stadium.*

zero. The number associated with the *empty set.* It is denoted by 0.

zero in division. Suppose a is a number other than zero. There are three possibilities:

$$1.\frac{0}{a} \quad 2.\frac{a}{0} \quad 3.\frac{0}{0}$$

1. $\frac{0}{a} = c$ means $a \times c = 0$.

Since $a \neq 0$, then $c = 0$.

Therefore, $\frac{0}{a} = 0$.

2. $\frac{a}{0} = c$ means $a = 0 \times c$.

But $0 \times c = 0$ for all numbers and cannot equal a, which is not zero. Therefore, $\frac{a}{0}$ is meaningless.

3. $\frac{0}{0} = n$ means $0 = 0 \times n$.

But this is true for any number n. For this reason, we say $\frac{0}{0}$ is indeterminate. Division by zero cannot be done. See *zero property of addition, zero in multiplication, additive identity.*

zero in multiplication. The product of zero and any number is zero. For all numbers, a, $a \times 0 = 0 \times a = 0$. For example, $125 \times 0 = 0 \times 125 = 0$.

zero point. That point on a *number line* associated with zero. It separates the points

$$\xleftarrow{\quad} \overset{\text{-3-2-1}}{} \overset{0}{\underset{\uparrow}{}} \overset{\text{+1+2+3}}{} \xrightarrow{\quad}$$
ZERO POINT

associated with the *positive numbers* on the right and the *negative numbers* on the left.

zero power. The value of any *real number* except that zero raised to the zero *power* is always 1. Any number with an *exponent* of zero is $1:3^0 = 1$;

$$127. 50^0 = 1; \left(\frac{15}{27}\right)^0 = 1.$$

For any real number a, $a^0 = 1$, where $a \neq 0$.

zero property of addition. There exists a *unique* number, zero, such that for any number a, $a + 0 = 0 + a = a$. For example, $6 + 0 = 0 + 6 = 6$. Zero is called the *additive identity* in addition.

zone. In geometry, the part of the surface of a *sphere* bounded by the two intersections of *parallel planes* with the sphere.

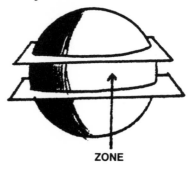

ZONE

TABLE OF SOME COMMONLY USED
MATHEMATICAL SYMBOLS

$+$	plus; add; positive
$-$	minus; subtract; negative
$\pm$	plus or minus
$\times$	times; multiply; cross
$\cdot$	times; multiply
$\div$	divide
$\overline{)}$	divide
$-,/$	divided by (as $\dfrac{a}{b}$)
$0,*$	undefined operation
$\sqrt{}$	square root
$\sqrt[3]{}$	cube root
$\sqrt[n]{}$	nth root
$\ldots$	between two numerals or letters, omission; at the end of a series or sequence, and so on
$\angle$	angle
$\triangle$	triangle (see also table of Greek letters used as symbols)
$\square$	rectangle
$\diamond$	parallelogram
$\odot$	circle
$\frown$	arc (as $\overset{\frown}{ABC}$)
$\overline{}$	line segment (as $\overline{AB}$)
$\leftrightarrow$	line
$\rightarrow$	ray
$\nearrow$	directed line segment
$\rightharpoonup$	vector
$\perp$	perpendicular
$\parallel$	parallel
$\circ$	degree
$=$	equals
$\neq$	is not equal to
$<$	is less than
$>$	is greater than
$\leq$	is less than or equal to
$\geq$	is greater than or equal to
$\approx$	is approximately equal to

$\sim$	is similar to
$\sim$	not (used as a connective)
$\equiv$	is identical to, in numbers
$\cong$	is congruent to, in figures
$\cap$	intersection; cap; meet
$\cup$	union; cup; join
{ }	encloses a set, when numbers are included; empty set when empty
),[ ]	operate on first, or as a group
|	such that
:	such that; is to
::	as
$\therefore$	therefore
$\subset$	is included in; is a subset of
$\not\subset$	is not included in; is not a subset of
|n|	absolute value of n
[ )	half-closed interval
( ]	half-open interval
%	percent
!	factorial
$\prime$	foot; minute
$\prime\prime$	inch; second
∞	infinity
$\circ$	open point
$\bullet$	closed point

Letters Used as Symbols for Sets and Subsets

C	the set of counting numbers
D	the set of real numbers
I	the set of integers
I_n	the set of negative integers
I_p	the set of positive integers
N	the set of natural numbers
R	the set of rational numbers
$\overline{R}$	the set of irrational numbers
R_a	the set of rational numbers of arithmetic

Greek Letters Commonly Used as Symbols

α	(alpha) to denote first in a series
β	(beta) to denote second in a series
γ	(gamma) to denote interior angle
Δ	(delta) with a variable to denote a small increase in the value of the variable
$\in$	(epsilon) stands for "is a member of"
$\notin$	(epsilon) stands for "is not a member of"
θ	(theta) stands for "any angle"
π	(pi) equals 3.1416 . . .
ε	(sigma) stands for "summation"
σ	(sigma) stands for "the sum of the divisors"
ϕ	(phi) sometimes stands for "empty set"
ρ	(rho) stands for "first element in ordered pair of polar coordinates"

TABLE OF SOME COMMONLY USED FORMULAS

Symbols used in formulas unless otherwise indicated.

A	area
a	altitude, apothem
B	area of a base
b₁, b₂	measure of bases
C	Celsius
c	circumference
d	diameter
e	measure of an edge
h	height and the symbol for Planck's constant
l	length
n	number of sides
p	perimeter
r	measure of a radius
S	surface area
s	measure of a side
V	volume
w	width
π	pi

Formulas for Plane Figures

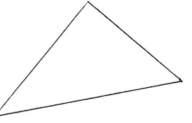

CIRCLE
circumference: $c = 2\pi r$; $c = \pi d$

area: $A = \pi r^2$; $A = \left(\dfrac{d}{2}\right)^2 \cdot \pi$

ELLIPSE
area: $A = \frac{1}{2}$ length of major axis $\times \frac{1}{2}$ length of minor axis) $\times \pi$

PARALLELOGRAM
area: $A = ab$

RECTANGLE
perimeter: $p = 2(1 + w)$
area: $A = lw$

REGULAR POLYGON
perimeter: $p = ns$
area: $A = \frac{1}{2}$ ans; $A = \frac{1}{2}$ ap

SQUARE
perimeter: $p = 4s$
area: $A = lw$; $A = s^2$

TRAPEZOID
area: $A = \frac{1}{2}(b_1 + b_2)$

TRIANGLE
area: $A = \frac{1}{2}ab$
perimeter: Where a, b and c are the measure of the sides:
$p = a + b + c$

EQUILATERAL TRIANGLE
perimeter: $p = 3s$

PYTHAGOREAN PROPERTY
Where c = hypotenuse and a and b = the measure of the sides
opposite the acute angles of a right triangle: $c^2 = a^2 + b^2$

Formulas for Space Figures

RIGHT CIRCULAR CONE
Where r = the measure of a radius of the base:
volume: $V = \frac{1}{3}$ Bh; $V = \frac{1}{3} \pi r^2 h$

CUBE
surface: $S = 6e^2$
volume: $V = e^3$

RIGHT CIRCULAR CYLINDER
Where r = the measure of a radius of a base:
surface: $S = 2\pi r(r + h)$
volume: $V = \pi r^2 h$

RECTANGULAR RIGHT PRISM
surface: $S = 2(lw + hw + lh)$
volume: $V = lwh$

RIGHT PRISM
volume: $V = Bh$
Where a = the measure of an apothem of a base: $V = \frac{1}{2}$ aph

TRIANGULAR RIGHT PRISM
Where a = the measure of an altitude of a triangle that determines the base, b = measure of the base of the triangle:
surface: $S = ab + hp$
volume: $V = \frac{1}{2}$ abh

REGULAR PYRAMID
Where a = the measure of an apothem of the base and p = the perimeter of the base:
volume: $V = \frac{1}{3}$ Bh; $V = \frac{1}{6}$ aph

SQUARE REGULAR PYRAMID
volume: $V = \frac{1}{3} (e^2 h)$

TRIANGULAR PYRAMID
Where a = the measure of an altitude of the triangle that determines the base, and b = the measure of the base:
volume: $V = \frac{1}{6}$ abh

SPHERE
surface: $S = 4\pi r^2$
volume: $V = \frac{4}{3}\pi r^3$

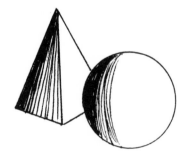

Formulas for Computations

AMOUNT
Where a = total amount, p = principal and i = interest: $a = p + i$

AVERAGE
Where a = average, t = total and n = number of items: $a = \dfrac{t}{n}$

COST
Where c = total cost, n = number of items and p = price of each item: $c = np$.
For finding the price of a single item when the total cost is known:

$$p = \frac{c}{n}$$

DISTANCE
Where d = distance, r = rate and t = time: $d = r\,t$
For falling objects: $d = 16t^2$

INTEREST
Where i = interest, p = principal, r = rate and t = time: $i = prt$

PERCENTAGE
Where p = percentage, b = base and r = rate: $p = br$

SELLING PRICE
Where s = selling price, c = cost, o = overhead and p = profit: $s = c + o + p$

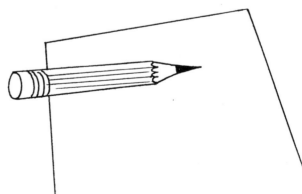

TABLES OF WEIGHTS AND MEASURES

AVOIRDUPOIS WEIGHT

27¹¹/₃₂ grains (gr.)	1 dram (dr.)
16 drams	1 ounce (oz.), 437½ grains
16 ounces	1 pound (lb.), 256 drams, 7,000 grains
100 pounds	1 hundredweight (cwt.), 1,600 ounces
112 pounds	1 long hundredweight (1.cwt.)
20 hundredweight	1 ton (t.), 2,000 pounds
20 long hundredweight	1 long ton (t.), 2,240 pounds

TROY WEIGHT

24 grains (gr.)	1 pennyweight (dwt.)
20 pennyweights	1 ounce (oz. t.) 480 grains
12 ounces	1 pound (lb. t.), 240 pennyweights, 5,760 grains

APOTHECARIES' WEIGHT

20 grains (gr.)	1 scruple (s. ap. or Ə)
3 scruples	1 dram (dr. ap. or ʒ), 60 grains
8 drams	1 ounce (oz. ap. or ʒ), 24 scruples, 480 grains
12 ounces	1 pound (lb. ap. or lb), 96 drams, 288 scruples, 5,760 grains)

LINEAR MEASURE

12 inches (in.)	1 foot (ft.)
3 feet	1 yard (yd.), 36 inches
5½ yards	1 rod (rd.), 16½ feet
40 rods	1 furlong (fur.), 220 yards, 660 feet
1 mile	5,280 feet
8 furlongs	1 statute mile (mi.), 1,760 yards, 5,280 feet
3 miles	1 league (1.), 5,280 yards.

SQUARE MEASURE

144 square inches (sq. in.). . 1 square foot (sq. ft.)

9 square feet . . . . 1 square yard (sq. yd.), 1,296 square inches

30¼ square yards . . . . 1 square rod (sq. rd.), 272¼ square feet

160 square rods. . . . . 1 acre (A.), 4,840 square yards

640 acres . . . . 1 square mile (sq. mi.), 3,097,600 square yards

36 square miles . . . . 1 township

CUBIC MEASURE

1,728 cubic inches (cu. in.) 1 cubic foot (cu. ft.)

27 cubic feet . . . . 1 cubic yard (cu. yd.)

144 cubic inches . . . . 1 board foot

128 cubic feet . . . . 1 cord

CHAIN MEASURE   Gunter's, or Surveyor's, Chain

7.92 inches (in.) . . . . 1 link (li.)

100 links . . . . 1 chain (ch.)

80 chains . . . . 1 mile (mi.)

                                     Engineer's Chain

12 inches . . . . 1 link

100 links . . . . 1 chain

52.8 chains . . . . 1 mile

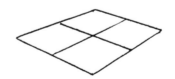

SURVEYOR'S AREA MEASURE

625 square links (sq. li.) ...	1 square rod or square pole (sq. p.)
16 square rods............	1 square chain (sq. ch.), surveyor's
10 square chains..........	1 acre (A.)
640 acres...............	1 square mile (sq. mi.)
36 square miles..........	1 township

LIQUID MEASURE

4 gills (gi.)..............	1 pint (pt.)
2 pints.................	1 quart (qt.), 8 gills
4 quarts................	1 gallon (gal.), 8 pints, 32 gills
31½ gallons	1 barrel (bbl.), 126 quarts
2 barrels	1 hogshead (hhd.), 63 gallons, 252 quarts

APOTHECARIES' FLUID MEASURE

60 minims (min. or ♏)	1 fluid dram (fl. dr. or f℥)
8 fluid drams............	1 fluid ounce (fl. oz. or f℥), 480 minims
16 fluid ounces	1 pint (o.), 128 fluid drams, 7,680 minims
8 pints	1 gallon (C.), 128 fluid ounces, 1,024 fluid drams

DRY MEASURE

2 pints (pt.).............	1 quart (qt.)
8 quarts	1 peck (pk.), 16 pints
4 pecks	1 bushel (bu.), 32 quarts, 64 pints
105 quarts	1 barrel (bbl.), dry measure, 7,056 cubic inches

ANGULAR AND CIRCULAR MEASURE

60 seconds (″)	1 minute (′)
60 minutes	1 degree (°)
90 degrees	1 quadrant (quad.)
180 degrees	1 straight angle
4 quadrants	1 circle

NAUTICAL MEASURE

6 feet	1 fathom (fath.)
100 fathoms	1 cable's length (ordinary)
120 fathoms	1 cable's length (U.S. Navy)
10 cable lengths	1 nautical mile
1 nautical mile	1.1515 statute miles
60 nautical miles	1 degree (deg. or °)
1 knot	1 nautical mile per hour

THE METRIC SYSTEM

LINEAR MEASURE
10 millimeters . . . .   1 centimeter
10 centimeters . . . .   1 decimeter
10 decimeters . . . .   1 meter
10 meters . . . .   1 decameter
10 decameters . . . .   1 hectometer
10 hectometers . . . .   1 kilometer

SQUARE MEASURE
100 sq. millimeters . . . .   1 sq. centimeter
100 sq. centimeters . . . .   1 sq. decimeter
100 sq. decimeters . . . .   1 sq. meter
100 sq. meters . . . .   1 sq. decameter
100 sq. decameters . . . .   1 sq. hectometer
100 sq. hectometers . . . .   1 sq. kilometer

CUBIC MEASURE
1000 cu. millimeters . . . .   1 cu. centimeter
1000 cu. centimeters . . . . . .   1 cu. decimeter
1000 cu. decimeters . . . .   1 cu. meter

LIQUID MEASURE
10 milliliters . . . .   1 centiliter
10 centiliters . . . .   1 deciliter
10 deciliters . . . .   1 liter
10 liters . . . .   1 decaliter
10 decaliters . . . .   1 hectoliter
10 hectoliters . . . .   1 kiloliter

WEIGHTS
10 milligrams . . . .   1 centigram
10 centigrams . . . .   1 decigram
10 decigrams . . . .   1 gram
10 grams . . . .   1 decagram
10 decagrams . . . .   1 hectogram
10 hectograms . . . .   1 kilogram
100 kilograms . . . .   1 quintal
10 quintals . . . .   1 ton

CONVERSION TABLE—METRIC AND ENGLISH SYSTEMS

centimeter	0.3937 inch
meter	39.37 inches (exactly)
square centimeters	.1549997 square inch
square meter	1.195985 square yards
hectare	2.47104 acres
cubic meter	1.3079428 cubic yards
liter	.264178 gallon
liter	1.05671 liquid quarts
liter	.908102 dry quart
hectoliter	2.83782 bushels
gram	15.432356 grains
kilogram	2.204622341 pounds, avoirdupois
inch	2.540005 centimeters
yard	.9144018 meter
mile	1.6094 kilometers
square inch	6.451626 square centimeters
square yard	.8361307 square meter
acre	.404687 hectare
cubic yard	.7645594 cubic meter
gallon	3.785332 liters
liquid quart	.946333 liter
dry quart	1.101198 liters
bushel	35.23833 liters
grain	.064798918 gram
pound, avoirdupois	.45359237 kilogram

PERIODIC TABLE OF THE CHEMICAL ELEMENTS

Group→ Period ↓	I	II							
1	1.0080 **H** 1								
2	6.939 **Li** 3	9.012 **Be** 4							
3	22.990 **Na** 11	24.32 **Mg** 12							
4	39.10 **K** 19	40.08 **Ca** 20	44.96 **Sc** 21	47.90 **Ti** 22	50.94 **V** 23	52.00 **Cr** 24	54.94 **Mn** 25	55.85 **Fe** 26	58.93 **Co** 27
5	85.47 **Rb** 37	87.62 **Sr** 38	88.91 **Y** 39	91.22 **Zr** 40	92.91 **Nb** 41	95.94 **Mo** 42	(99) **Tc** 43	101.07 **Ru** 44	102.91 **Rh** 45
6	132.91 **Cs** 55	137.34 **Ba** 56	* 57-71	178.49 **Hf** 72	180.95 **Ta** 73	183.85 **W** 74	186.2 **Re** 75	190.2 **Os** 76	192.2 **Ir** 77
7	(223) **Fr** 87	226.05 **Ra** 88	† 89-103	(261) **Rf** 104	(260) **Ha** 105	(263) 106	etc.		

*Rare-earth metals	138.91 **La** 57	140.12 **Ce** 58	140.91 **Pr** 59	144.27 **Nd** 60	(147) **Pm** 61
†Actinide metals	(227) **Ac** 89	232.04 **Th** 90	(231) **Pa** 91	238.03 **U** 92	(237) **Np** 93

			III	IV	V	VI	VII	0
								4.0026 **He** 2
			10.811 **B** 5	12.011 **C** 6	14.007 **N** 7	15.999 **O** 8	18.998 **F** 9	20.183 **Ne** 10
			26.98 **Al** 13	28.09 **Si** 14	30.97 **P** 15	32.06 **S** 16	35.45 **Cl** 17	39.95 **Ar** 18
3.71 **Ni** 28	63.54 **Cu** 29	65.37 **Zn** 30	69.72 **Ga** 31	72.59 **Ge** 32	74.92 **As** 33	78.96 **Se** 34	79.91 **Br** 35	83.80 **Kr** 36
06.4 **Pd** 46	107.87 **Ag** 47	112.40 **Cd** 48	114.82 **In** 49	118.69 **Sn** 50	121.75 **Sb** 51	127.60 **Te** 52	126.9 **I** 53	131.30 **Xe** 54
5.09 **Pt** 78	196.97 **Au** 79	200.59 **Hg** 80	204.37 **Tl** 81	207.19 **Pb** 82	208.98 **Bi** 83	(210) **Po** 84	(210) **At** 85	222 **Rn** 86

Atomic mass (A)
Abbreviation for element
Atomic number (Z)

0.35 **Sm** 62	151.96 **Eu** 63	157.25 **Gd** 64	158.92 **Tb** 65	162.50 **Dy** 66	164.93 **Ho** 67	167.26 **Er** 68	168.93 **Tm** 69	173.04 **Yb** 70	174.97 **Lu** 71
242) **Pu** 94	(243) **Am** 95	(245) **Cm** 96	(249) **Bk** 97	(249) **Cf** 98	(253) **E** 99	(255) **Fm** 100	(256) **Mv** 101	(253) **No** 102	(257) **Lr** 103

TABLE OF SQUARE ROOTS

N	√N	N	√N	N	√N	N	√N	N	√N	N	√N
1	1.000	51	7.141	101	10.050	151	12.288	201	14.177	251	15.843
2	1.414	52	7.211	102	10.100	152	12.329	202	14.213	252	15.875
3	1.732	53	7.280	103	10.149	153	12.369	203	14.248	253	15.906
4	2.000	54	7.348	104	10.198	154	12.410	204	14.283	254	15.937
5	2.236	55	7.416	105	10.247	155	12.450	205	14.318	255	15.969
6	2.449	56	7.483	106	10.296	156	12.490	206	14.353	256	16.000
7	2.646	57	7.550	107	10.344	157	12.530	207	14.388	257	16.031
8	2.828	58	7.616	108	10.392	158	12.570	208	14.422	258	16.062
9	3.000	59	7.681	109	10.440	159	12.610	209	14.457	259	16.093
10	3.162	60	7.746	110	10.488	160	12.649	210	14.491	260	16.124
11	3.317	61	7.810	111	10.536	161	12.689	211	14.526	261	16.155
12	3.464	62	7.874	112	10.583	162	12.728	212	14.560	262	16.186
13	3.606	63	7.937	113	10.630	163	12.767	213	14.595	263	16.217
14	3.742	64	8.000	114	10.677	164	12.806	214	14.629	264	16.248
15	3.873	65	8.062	115	10.724	165	12.845	215	14.663	265	16.279
16	4.000	66	8.124	116	10.770	166	12.884	216	14.697	266	16.310
17	4.123	67	8.185	117	10.817	167	12.923	217	14.731	267	16.340
18	4.243	68	8.246	118	10.863	168	12.962	218	14.765	268	16.371
19	4.359	69	8.307	119	10.909	169	13.000	219	14.799	269	16.401
20	4.472	70	8.367	120	10.955	170	13.038	220	14.832	270	16.432
21	4.583	71	8.426	121	11.000	171	13.077	221	14.866	271	16.462
22	4.690	72	8.485	122	11.045	172	13.115	222	14.900	272	16.492
23	4.796	73	8.544	123	11.091	173	13.153	223	14.933	273	16.523
24	4.899	74	8.602	124	11.136	174	13.191	224	14.967	274	16.553
25	5.000	75	8.660	125	11.180	175	13.229	225	15.000	275	16.583
26	5.099	76	8.718	126	11.225	176	13.267	226	15.033	276	16.613
27	5.196	77	8.775	127	11.269	177	13.304	227	15.067	277	16.643
28	5.292	78	8.832	128	11.314	178	13.342	228	15.100	278	16.673
29	5.385	79	8.888	129	11.358	179	13.379	229	15.133	279	16.703
30	5.477	80	8.944	130	11.402	180	13.416	230	15.166	280	16.733
31	5.568	81	9.000	131	11.446	181	13.454	231	15.199	281	16.763
32	5.657	82	9.055	132	11.489	182	13.491	232	15.232	282	16.793
33	5.745	83	9.110	133	11.533	183	13.528	233	15.264	283	16.823
34	5.831	84	9.165	134	11.576	184	13.565	234	15.297	284	16.852
35	5.916	85	9.220	135	11.619	185	13.602	235	15.330	285	16.882
36	6.000	86	9.274	136	11.662	186	13.638	236	15.362	286	16.912
37	6.083	87	9.327	137	11.705	187	13.675	237	15.395	287	16.941
38	6.164	88	9.381	138	11.747	188	13.711	238	15.427	288	16.971
39	6.245	89	9.434	139	11.790	189	13.748	239	15.460	289	17.000
40	6.325	90	9.487	140	11.832	190	13.784	240	15.492	290	17.029
41	6.403	91	9.539	141	11.874	191	13.820	241	15.524	291	17.059
42	6.481	92	9.592	142	11.916	192	13.856	242	15.556	292	17.088
43	6.557	93	9.644	143	11.958	193	13.892	243	15.588	293	17.117
44	6.633	94	9.695	144	12.000	194	13.928	244	15.620	294	17.146
45	6.708	95	9.741	145	12.042	195	13.964	245	15.652	295	17.176
46	6.782	96	9.798	146	12.083	196	14.000	246	15.684	296	17.205
47	6.856	97	9.849	147	12.124	197	14.036	247	15.716	297	17.234
48	6.928	98	9.899	148	12.166	198	14.071	248	15.748	298	17.263
49	7.000	99	9.950	149	12.207	199	14.107	249	15.780	299	17.292
50	7.071	100	10.000	150	12.247	200	14.142	250	15.811	300	17.321

LOGARITHM TABLE

log π = .4971   log 4 π = 1.0992   log ⅓ π = .6221

N	0	1	2	3	4	5	6	7	8	9
10	0000	0043	0086	0128	0170	0212	0253	0294	0334	0374
11	0414	0453	0492	0531	0569	0607	0645	0682	0719	0755
12	0792	0828	0864	0899	0934	0969	1004	1038	1072	1106
13	1139	1173	1206	1239	1271	1303	1335	1367	1399	1430
14	1461	1492	1523	1553	1584	1614	1644	1673	1703	1732
15	1761	1790	1818	1847	1875	1903	1931	1959	1987	2014
16	2041	2068	2095	2122	2148	2175	2201	2227	2253	2279
17	2304	2330	2355	2380	2405	2430	2455	2480	2504	2529
18	2553	2577	2601	2625	2648	2672	2695	2718	2742	2765
19	2788	2810	2833	2856	2878	2900	2923	2945	2967	2989
20	3010	3032	3054	3075	3096	3118	3139	3160	3181	3201
21	3222	3243	3263	3284	3304	3324	3345	3365	3385	3404
22	3424	3444	3464	3483	3502	3522	3541	3560	3579	3598
23	3617	3636	3655	3674	3692	3711	3729	3747	3766	3784
24	3802	3820	3838	3856	3874	3892	3909	3927	3945	3962
25	3979	3997	4014	4031	4048	4065	4082	4099	4116	4133
26	4150	4166	4183	4200	4216	4232	4249	4265	4281	4298
27	4314	4330	4346	4362	4378	4393	4409	4425	4440	4456
28	4472	4487	4502	4518	4533	4548	4564	4579	4594	4609
29	4624	4639	4654	4669	4683	4698	4713	4728	4742	4757
30	4771	4786	4800	4814	4829	4843	4857	4871	4886	4900
31	4914	4928	4942	4955	4969	4983	4997	5011	5024	5038
32	5051	5065	5079	5092	5105	5119	5132	5145	5159	5172
33	5185	5198	5211	5224	5237	5250	5263	5276	5289	5302
34	5315	5328	5340	5353	5366	5378	5391	5403	5416	5428
35	5441	5453	5465	5478	5490	5502	5514	5527	5539	5551
36	5563	5575	5587	5599	5611	5623	5635	5647	5658	5670
37	5682	5694	5705	5717	5729	5740	5752	5763	5775	5786
38	5798	5809	5821	5832	5843	5855	5866	5877	5888	5899
39	5911	5922	5933	5944	5955	5966	5977	5988	5999	6010
40	6021	6031	6042	6053	6064	6075	6085	6096	6107	6117
41	6128	6138	6149	6160	6170	6180	6191	6201	6212	6222
42	6232	6243	6253	6263	6274	6284	6294	6304	6314	6325
43	6335	6345	6355	6365	6375	6385	6395	6405	6415	6425
44	6435	6444	6454	6464	6474	6484	6493	6503	6513	6522
45	6532	6542	6551	6561	6571	6580	6590	6599	6609	6618
46	6628	6637	6646	6656	6665	6675	6684	6693	6702	6712
47	6721	6730	6739	6749	6758	6767	6776	6785	6794	6803
48	6812	6821	6830	6839	6848	6857	6866	6875	6884	6893
49	6902	6911	6920	6928	6937	6946	6955	6964	6972	6981
50	6990	6998	7007	7016	7024	7033	7042	7050	7059	7067
51	7076	7084	7093	7101	7110	7118	7126	7135	7143	7152
52	7160	7168	7177	7185	7193	7202	7210	7218	7226	7235
53	7243	7251	7259	7267	7275	7284	7292	7300	7308	7316
54	7324	7332	7340	7348	7356	7364	7372	7380	7388	7396
N	0	1	2	3	4	5	6	7	8	9

LOGARITHM TABLE

log π = .4971   log 4 π = 1.0992   log ⅓ π = .6221

N	0	1	2	3	4	5	6	7	8	9
55	7404	7412	7419	7427	7435	7443	7451	7459	7466	7474
56	7482	7490	7497	7505	7513	7520	7528	7536	7543	7551
57	7559	7566	7574	7582	7589	7597	7604	7612	7619	7627
58	7634	7642	7649	7657	7664	7672	7679	7686	7694	7701
59	7709	7716	7723	7731	7738	7745	7752	7760	7767	7774
60	7782	7789	7796	7803	7810	7818	7825	7832	7839	7846
61	7853	7860	7868	7875	7882	7889	7896	7903	7910	7917
62	7924	7931	7938	7945	7952	7959	7966	7973	7980	7987
63	7993	8000	8007	8014	8021	8028	8035	8041	8048	8055
64	8062	8069	8075	8082	8089	8096	8102	8109	8116	8122
65	8129	8136	8142	8149	8156	8162	8169	8176	8182	8189
66	8195	8202	8209	8215	8222	8228	8235	8241	8248	8254
67	8261	8267	8274	8280	8287	8293	8299	8306	8312	8319
68	8325	8331	8338	8344	8351	8357	8363	8370	8376	8382
69	8388	8395	8401	8407	8414	8420	8426	8432	8439	8445
70	8451	8457	8463	8470	8476	8482	8488	8494	8500	8506
71	8513	8519	8525	8531	8537	8543	8549	8555	8561	8567
72	8573	8579	8585	8591	8597	8603	8609	8615	8621	8627
73	8633	8639	8645	8651	8657	8663	8669	8675	8681	8686
74	8692	8698	8704	8710	8716	8722	8727	8733	8739	8745
75	8751	8756	8762	8768	8774	8779	8785	8791	8797	8802
76	8808	8814	8820	8825	8831	8837	8842	8848	8854	8859
77	8865	8871	8876	8882	8887	8893	8899	8904	8910	8915
78	8921	8927	8932	8938	8943	8949	8954	8960	8965	8971
79	8976	8982	8987	8993	8998	9004	9009	9015	9020	9025
80	9031	9036	9042	9047	9053	9058	9063	9069	9074	9079
81	9095	9090	9096	9101	9106	9112	9117	9122	9128	9133
82	9138	9143	9149	9154	9159	9165	9170	9175	9180	9186
83	9191	9196	9201	9206	9212	9217	9222	9227	9232	9238
84	9243	9248	9253	9258	9263	9269	9274	9279	9284	9289
85	9294	9299	9304	9309	9315	9320	9325	9330	9335	9340
86	9345	9350	9355	9360	9365	9370	9375	9380	9385	9390
87	9395	9400	9405	9410	9415	9420	9425	9430	9435	9440
88	9445	9450	9455	9460	9465	9469	9474	9479	9484	9489
89	9494	9499	9504	9509	9513	9518	9523	9528	9533	9538
90	9542	9547	9552	9557	9562	9566	9571	9576	9581	9586
91	9590	9595	9600	9605	9609	9614	9619	9624	9628	9633
92	9638	9643	9647	9652	9657	9661	9666	9671	9675	9680
93	9685	9689	9694	9699	9703	9708	9713	9717	9722	9727
94	9731	9736	9741	9745	9750	9754	9759	9763	9768	9773
95	9777	9782	9786	9791	9795	9800	9805	9809	9814	9818
96	9823	9827	9832	9836	9841	9845	9850	9854	9859	9863
97	9868	9872	9877	9881	9886	9890	9894	9899	9903	9908
98	9912	9917	9921	9926	9930	9934	9939	9943	9948	9952
99	9956	9961	9965	9969	9974	9978	9938	9987	9991	9996
N	0	1	2	3	4	5	6	7	8	9

CHAPTER 2
LIVE OAK SCHOOL DISTRICT